Gourmet Cooking for Everyone

*For Robin, Jeremy and Angela, without
whose interest in eating, this book
would never have been written*

GOURMET COOKING FOR EVERYONE

❖❖❖

Guirne Van Zuylen

FABER AND FABER

3 Queen Square

London

First published in 1969
First published in this edition 1975
by Faber and Faber Limited
3 Queen Square London WC1
Printed in Great Britain by
Whitstable Litho, Straker Brothers Ltd

ISBN 0 571 10669 2 *(Faber Paper Covered Editions)*

ISBN 0 571 08714 0 *(hard bound edition)*

Contents

❉❉❉

Introduction

❖❖❖

Within the last ten years I think more nonsense has been written and talked about the mystique of cooking, and French cooking particularly, than with almost any other branch of the domestic arts.

Most English people are under the misapprehension that there is no such thing as bad cooking in France, and most French people that there is no such thing as good cooking in England. Of course both are wrong. I have eaten some really appalling meals in France, and some quite unforgettably good ones in England; and one of the most famous cooks in Bordeaux, one of the great gastronomic centres of France, near where I live, is an Englishwoman. Although France is still the fountainhead of the greatest culinary inventions, it is ridiculous to condemn every other country's cookery, and I must admit I am rather tired of the lengths to which this form of snobbery is carried.

Cooking is rather like painting. You learn the basic principles, you are advised on the mixing and use of colours, but in the end you evolve your own palette. I have yet to taste two dishes, prepared with the same ingredients by any two people, which come out precisely identical. In any case, it is not always possible to obtain exactly the ingredients given in the recipe. Very often it is possible to adapt a dish with no detriment to the result. Indeed, the different versions of many

Introduction

French regional dishes are the consequence of using what happens to be available.

I always consider my own culinary masterpiece was achieved in London during the last war, when I used to make Crêpes Mornay from powdered milk, dried eggs and war-time flour. Fried in medicinal oil to which, as an expectant mother, I was entitled, and filled with a Béchamel sauce, flavoured with the weekly cheese ration, they seemed truly epicurean, and I was far prouder of this *tour de force* than I could be of the most inspired creation today—particularly as we were living in a large and rather unpractical house, I had two babies, my only domestic help spent the greater part of her working day cowering in an air-raid shelter, and my shopping expeditions took anything up to three hours, standing in queues.

To be a good cook requires really only one qualification. You must enjoy eating, and the rest is common sense and imagination. Nowadays, when the whole set-up of our lives has been so simplified, it is possible to provide simple and beautifully cooked food with the minimum of troublesome preliminaries. Most people have too many other occupations to find the time to stand for hours in a hot kitchen, and most modern kitchens are not planned with the unlimited space required for elaborate confections involving the use of several saucepans and numerous other utensils. None of the recipes in this book requires lengthy, complicated or costly prepara-tions. Many can be cooked or partially cooked a day in ad-vance, so that a whole meal can be produced in an average of an hour to an hour and a half, and you need not be ashamed to serve any one of them to the most critical of epicures.

Try to choose your menus seasonally. For instance, when eggs are cheap is the time to serve mousses and soufflés, and sauces with egg yolks. Cream and milk are usually cheaper in the spring and summer.

I am not a great believer in out-of-season food. In France, which is a self-supporting country, there is very little frozen food, and not much imported food. Consequently the French tend to eat their vegetables and fruit in their right season, almost as soon as buds, pods and leaves have formed. The meat is all home produced, but the cuts are totally different from those in England. There are now butchers in London and other large cities who are beginning to provide French butchery which, though you may pay a little more for it, works out much more economically in the end, as there is no waste. In France when you buy meat, you state the dish you are going to make—a roast, a pot-au-feu, a daube—and the butcher prepares the appropriate cut accordingly.

When choosing your menu, try to arrange for at least one dish that can be prepared in advance, say the day before, and limit yourself to not more than three courses. Start with the preparation of those dishes which are going to take longest to cook, and do all the messy things first, such as washing and peeling vegetables, skinning and boning fish, so that you can clear all the unwanted bits and pieces away, and have a clean space to work on.

As long as you are systematic in your kitchen, you will not find yourself left with a pile of dirty saucepans, knives and so on, to dispose of before your guests arrive.

It is a real economy to buy first-class utensils, particularly saucepans. Cheap ones tend to burn or stick. My own personal preference is for aluminium, and I am still using the saucepans I had when I married, almost thirty years ago! I advise a minimum of four to start with: one big enough to boil a chicken, a piece of ham or bones for stock; two medium-sized ones; and a smaller one, with a double lip if possible, for sauces. If funds will run to it, get a double saucepan, invaluable for all mixtures cooked with egg.

A great deal has been written about frying pans and how essential it is to have a separate one for omelettes, pancakes and other egg-based dishes. But I promise that if you buy a really good quality one and keep it absolutely spotless with abrasive wool, you can use it for everything, except deep frying—and I have included no recipes for this form of cooking, for the good reason that in a small place the smell clings, even with wide open windows *and* an extractor fan, and there is nothing more calculated to turn your appetite than the smell of stale frying permeating a home.

The new flame-proof casserole dishes which can be used either on the top of the stove or in the oven are quite invaluable, as they can be brought straight to the table, and are saving on both space and washing-up. An oval or rectangular one is a good shape for meat or fish, and a round one with a lid can be used for a number of dishes needing slow cooking.

Here is a list of utensils which are really necessary:

A large and a small wooden spoon
A perforated slice for draining (an oblong shape is the most practical)
A palette knife
Two sharp knives, one with a short blade for vegetables, the other for cutting and trimming meat, etc. (I rather incline towards the serrated variety. They seem to need less sharpening)
A colander
A large and a small wire strainer
A vegetable peeler
An egg whisk

Introduction

A food mill (essential for purées of vegetables, fruit, etc.)
A smaller version for grating cheese or breadcrumbs
A grater
A tin opener
A couple of good baking tins
A liquid measure
Two or three mixing basins
A chopping board
A pair of scissors (I use mine for endless purposes—cutting up
  meat and fish, chopping parsley, shredding vegetables, to
  name only a few)
A rolling-pin (I have made do with a wine bottle, but the real
  thing gives better results!)

It has been my proud boast that I have never had to turn
the unexpected guest away; not because I have had a store
cupboard filled with rows of tins, nor because I have lived
almost next door to a delicatessen which could provide an
emergency meal from a deep freeze. I try to keep a supply of
ingredients which can be used in a variety of ways, and with
these and the very excellent dried herbs and spices which can
be obtained at most good grocers', you have the nucleus of
a number of attractive impromptu dishes.

I always keep flour, rice and spaghetti, and a packet of
haricot beans, and sometimes semolina or sago. Since the
appearance on the market of a number of excellent brands of
dehydrated vegetables, I keep a packet or two of these in reserve. A tube of concentrated tomato purée, a few bouillon
cubes and some dried prunes, raisins and currants are helpful
in dressing up the most unpromising beginning, and my
fridge is never without cheese and eggs.

Now for the herbs and spices. Don't buy large quantities, as
their strength tends to evaporate after a while and you are left

with a number of packets, all with a precisely similar aroma of dried grass. Here is my check-list:

Parsley	Basil
Thyme	Cloves
Bay leaves	Nutmeg
Marjoram or oregano	Cinnamon
Rosemary	Ginger

I have put parsley first: this should be used fresh whenever possible and is a most important flavouring, and not just a frilly green decoration as so many people seem to think. If you keep a little bunch in water in the fridge, it will last quite a long time.

Invest in a pepper mill. Freshly ground black pepper tastes totally different from the already ground stuff in cartons. There is as much difference as there is between buying coffee ready ground, and grinding the freshly roasted beans oneself.

In my recipes I have given most of the quantities in spoonfuls or cupfuls. In many kitchens there is no room for a pair of scales, and in any case they are a very expensive piece of equipment. You will probably find, once you become experienced, that your eye will be a pretty accurate judge of quantity.

A table of relative gas and electric oven temperatures will be found on page 150.

The kitchen is the one room in the house to which everyone gravitates. It seems to have an atmosphere of informality which can put the shyest guest at his ease. As one spends so much time in the kitchen, don't grudge the expense of making it as attractive and labour-saving as possible.

Hints and Warnings

❋✲❋✲❋✲❋✲❋✲❋✲❋✲❋✲❋✲❋✲❋✲❋✲❋✲❋✲❋✲❋✲❋✲❋✲❋✲❋

RICE

There are many theories on the most successful way to cook rice. Of course a great deal depends on the quality of the rice. For pilafs and risottos I try to use the plump yellow Italian kind, which can be bought at most continental stores. It separates beautifully, but if you cannot obtain it choose a long-grained Patna rice, which if properly cooked should be just as fluffy though the grain is smaller. I find the most fool-proof method for making sure you do not overcook your rice, and so produce a glutinous mass, is to put the required amount into a saucepan (a heaped tablespoonful per person and one or two over, according to appetites), cover with cold water to an inch above the rice, add salt and bring slowly to the boil. Put the lid on and cook gently till all the water is absorbed. Your rice should then be perfectly done, and all you need to do before serving is to strain it and run hot water through it for a minute or two, to separate the grains and get rid of the starch. If you are serving it as an accompaniment to meat or fish, dry it off by putting it into a cool oven for a few minutes.

While on the subject of rice, don't forget the difference between a pilaf and a risotto. In the first, the rice is boiled, and the butter or oil added after it is cooked. In the second the rice is sautéd in the fat (i.e. tossed lightly till partly cooked), and then cooked slowly enough to absorb the liquid, which is added little by little.

PASTA

Cook all pasta (spaghetti, macaroni, etc.), in very fast-boiling salted water, stirring from time to time to keep the strands separate and unstuck, and undercook rather than overcook. Strain without rinsing and serve immediately in a pre-heated dish with a good lump of butter, or a tablespoonful or two of olive oil, if you are not incorporating it with a sauce.

CREAM

Be careful not to whip cream too stiff or you may suddenly find it has turned to butter. It must remain light but inflated. Once it has started to thicken, slow down the beating, so that you can stop at just the right moment.

GELATINE

I find the best results with gelatine are obtained by dissolving it first in cold water (just enough to allow it to swell), then placing the cup, or whatever receptacle you have used, in a saucepan containing a little water and cooking gently till the mixture becomes syrupy. You can then strain it easily into whatever dish you are making. When adding gelatine to an already cold mixture, be careful to cool it off a little before combining the two; otherwise you may find the warm gelatine will turn lumpy when it comes in contact with the cold mixture. In this case, it is better to add the mixture to the gelatine rather than the reverse, and to add it gradually.

Hints and Warnings

CORNFLOUR

In order to make sure that your cornflour doesn't go lumpy in cooking, put the required amount into a cup or small basin, and to begin with add only enough liquid to make a smooth paste before combining with the mixture you wish to thicken.

EGG WHITES

The beating of egg whites can sometimes be tricky. When a recipe calls for egg whites to be stiffly beaten the right degree of stiffness can be judged when you can draw the consistency up into little peaks. (When I was a young girl we were taught to beat the whites on a plate with a fork till they were sufficiently stiff to remain on the plate when it was turned upside down.) Don't overbeat, or the whites will become too grainy to amalgamate with the other ingredients.

VINEGAR AND OIL

Don't ever use anything but wine vinegar. Malt vinegar is too harsh. And be sparing even with wine vinegar in both salad dressing and mayonnaise. Use both olive oil and a good nut oil in the kitchen. Olive oil is ideal for those meat dishes which require long cooking or a marinade to start with, and it gives flavour to salads. I always use nut oil for mayonnaise, and for frying. Incidentally, although most cookery books advise for a salad dressing one part of vinegar to three parts of oil, I find this too strong and use one part of vinegar to five or six parts of oil. In this case use more salt.

WINE IN COOKING

It is an absolutely mistaken idea that cooking with wine is a wasteful extravagance. Believe me, it works out far cheaper than buying endless bottles of sauces and other artificial flavourings, which are usually so highly seasoned that they are almost guaranteed to kill the flavour of anything.

Wine, on the contrary, helps to bring it out. A sauce made with white wine will bring distinction to the cheapest fish dish, and red wine in a meat stew will not only help to tenderize a cheap cut of meat, but will certainly bring out the flavour of all the ingredients. Never, for such dishes, *add* wine at the end. The important thing to remember is that the wine must be cooked so that the alcohol evaporates.

You don't need to buy an expensive wine, and if you keep it well corked it should retain its strength and flavour. It is not a bad idea, if you do not often cook with wine, to buy half bottles. The total difference in cost is negligible. I also keep a quarter bottle of brandy and a sample size of kirsch or maraschino. A spoonful of either of these does wonders for the most uninteresting dish of stewed fruit.

MAYONNAISE

Just a word of warning. Never put home-made mayonnaise into the fridge. The contrast of the warmer air after the coldness of the ice box will invariably cause it to curdle. If you are not going to use it straight away, cover with a plate and leave it in an even temperature away from draughts.

VEGETABLES

The general rule for the cooking of vegetables by boiling is to put the root vegetables into cold water, bring to the boil and cook slowly. With the leaves and pods it is just the contrary, they must be put into boiling water and cooked fast. In both cases, undercook rather than overcook. Nothing is nastier than khaki-coloured cabbage looking and tasting like old rags, or carrots which arrive at the table with the consistency of stewed cotton wool.

BREADCRUMBS

For recipes needing breadcrumbs, if you have no bread stale enough, or no time to sieve, put the equivalent amount of bread (without the crusts) into a basin and pour on just enough boiling water for the bread to absorb without becoming mushy. Then put a plate on the top for 5–10 minutes. The steam will add enough moisture to the bread to enable you to beat it up easily with a fork, before mixing with your other ingredients.

Soups

Bouillon • Beetroot soup • Cream of barley • Cream of carrots • Potage aux légumes • Potage à la dauphinoise • Leek and potato soup • Lentil soup • Cream of lettuce • Cream of mushroom • Soupe à l'oignon • Potage maigre • Potage Parmentier • Cream of tomato • Watercress soup • Vichyssoise

Soups

Not so long ago no soup was considered complete without a basis of meat stock. Nowadays people are realizing that in many vegetable soups stock kills the delicate flavour of young vegetables. However, a good bouillon can form the basis not only of consommé but of certain sauces. So I will start this chapter with a recipe for bouillon.

BOUILLON

To 3 quarts of water:

1 large carrot cut into 2 or 3 pieces	2 or 3 rashers of bacon
1 medium-sized onion	A bouquet of parsley stalks, thyme and bay leaf
3 lb. beef and veal bones	Salt and 12 peppercorns
1 lb. shin of beef	

Simmer on the lowest-possible gas for 4–5 hours, or you can leave it on all night if well covered. Strain and leave to go cold. Remove fat, and clarify by bringing again slowly to the boil with two slightly-beaten whites of eggs. This should be sufficient for the liquid in the saucepan, which will have reduced during cooking by at least a pint. Simmer for 15 minutes, turn off the heat and leave for another 15 minutes before straining through a cloth. With a boiling-up every day or two this stock will keep for a week in the fridge.

Soups

BEETROOT SOUP

This is a most delicious soup when beetroots are young. Melt an ounce of butter and fry in it a small well-chopped onion. When this is soft, stir in a tablespoonful of flour and add 1½–2 pints of stock. Bring to the boil, and go on stirring for 5 minutes. Cover and simmer for 20 minutes. Peel and slice 1 large or 2 medium-sized beetroots, lay the slices in a shallow dish, sprinkle them with salt and pepper and add enough vinegar just to cover them. Leave for a minute or two, then take them out and drop them into the soup. Cook for another 15 minutes (not longer or you will spoil the colour), then put the soup through the finest mesh of the food mill, but include only half the beetroot. Bring to the boil again and just before serving stir in 3 or 4 tablespoonfuls of cream. Add a sprinkling of either watercress leaves or coarsely-chopped parsley.

CREAM OF BARLEY

Well wash a heaped tablespoonful of pearl barley and put it into a saucepan with a quart of stock. Cover, and simmer for an hour. The barley should by this time be soft enough to pass easily through the food mill. Return to the saucepan, add a good scraping of nutmeg, check seasoning and bring again to the boil. Now add a pinch of sugar, 1½ oz. butter and a carton of cream (containing approximately a gill). Serve with fried croûtons (little squares of bread, fried crisp in very hot oil).

CREAM OF CARROTS

Peel and slice half a dozen medium-sized carrots. Wash well, put into cold water with salt and bring to the boil. Let them boil fairly fast for 5 minutes, then drain them. Put them back into the saucepan with 2 oz. butter, a medium-sized onion chopped small and a sliced leek. Stir for a few moments, then add 2 pints of stock, salt, pepper and a grating of nutmeg. When the carrots are soft enough to be mashed against the side of the saucepan with a fork, put the soup through the food mill. Add a teaspoonful of sugar and a level tablespoonful of cornflour dissolved in a teacupful of milk. Bring to the boil again and if the soup seems too thick, thin down by adding more stock. Serve with a couple of tablespoonfuls of rice, previously boiled, a sprinkling of parsley and a few drops of vinegar.

POTAGE AUX LÉGUMES

This is one of the many varieties of Garbure, a traditional soup of the Landes. Most versions include pieces of sausage, bacon and often goose, so that it becomes a sort of stew and very filling. This version, however, is much simpler. I have eaten it as a most comforting first course in the winter.

Fry gently in butter a medium-sized onion, 2 leeks, 2 carrots, 2 large tomatoes and 2 rashers of bacon, chopped. When the vegetables are beginning to get soft add 2½ pints of stock, a stick of celery cut into ½ inch pieces and 3 leaves of young cabbage well shredded. Leave to simmer for 20 minutes, when the vegetables should be almost cooked. Throw in a handful of peas and cook for a further 10 minutes.

POTAGE À LA DAUPHINOISE

When turnips are young, this makes a nice change. Wash and peel 4 small turnips, 4 small potatoes and 3 leeks. Slice them and put them in a saucepan with 2 oz. butter. Cover and let them sweat until soft, stirring occasionally. Season with salt, pepper and a grating of nutmeg and add 2 pints of white (chicken or veal) stock. Cook slowly until tender enough to pass through the food mill, stir in a carton of cream and serve with fried croûtons.

LEEK AND POTATO SOUP

A very simple soup, which can be prepared in under half an hour.

Cut 4 medium leeks into rounds after washing well and removing the tough outside leaves and hairy roots. Peel and cut similarly 4 potatoes. Sweat the slices in butter or margarine, stirring from time to time to make sure they do not stick to the bottom of the pan. Add seasoning, and when they are becoming soft, pour in 1½ pints of cold water. Finish cooking gently with the lid on (about 10 minutes). When done, mash the vegetables against the side of the saucepan with a fork, and before serving add ½ pint of milk, and reheat, then add a tablespoonful or two of cream if you have it, otherwise use a small piece of butter. This soup should not be smooth, but have a lumpy consistency.

LENTIL SOUP

When you have boiled a piece of ham, keep the stock and use it for this unusual soup.

Wash and slice a medium-sized onion and sweat it in 2 oz. butter. Add 4 tablespoonfuls of red lentils, turning them well over in the butter until all are well coated. Pour on your stock and leave to cook gently for 15 minutes, when the soup should be soft enough to pass through the finest mesh of the food mill. It should now be a smooth cream. Serve with a few spoonfuls of cream, or top of the milk, and plenty of parsley, stirred in at the last moment.

CREAM OF LETTUCE

When lettuces are cheap or running to seed, here is a way to use them up. Shred two lettuces finely and wash and drain well. Put them in a saucepan with 1½ oz. butter and sweat them till soft. Add 1½ pints of chicken stock (or a bouillon cube) and a heaped tablespoonful of rice, and simmer very slowly till cooked. Put through a sieve and serve with croûtons. This soup is also delicious cold, with a spoonful or two of cream stirred in at the last moment. In this case, leave out the croûtons.

CREAM OF MUSHROOM

Slice thinly 6 oz. mushrooms and fry gently, together with a small finely sliced onion, in 2 oz. butter. Add a tablespoonful of flour and stir vigorously till the mixture leaves the sides of the pan. Season and pour in slowly, stirring all the time, 1½ pints of stock. Continue cooking for another 10 minutes, when the soup should look creamy. Just before serving stir in a few tablespoonfuls of cream and a good handful of chopped parsley.

SOUPE À L'OIGNON

This most classic of soups, which with slight variations is eaten all over France, is warming, inexpensive and, if there is nothing else available, a meal in itself.

Allow 1 large onion per person. Peel and slice into rings and cook very gently in butter, stirring constantly. When just golden, add 2½ pts. stock (to 6 onions) gradually; bring slowly to the boil. Lower the heat, cover the pan and simmer for 45 minutes. Check the seasoning and when ready to serve, cut slices of bread into rounds so that they exactly fit the bowls. (If you have no bowls, breakfast cups are quite a good substitute.) Toast and butter the rounds. Pour out the soup, fit in the toasted lids, cover with a heaped serving of grated cheese (Gruyère for preference, as it gives the authentic slightly sweet flavour) and brown under the grill till the cheese is well melted.

POTAGE MAIGRE

The French, who so often suffer from liver disturbances, use this soup when they are dieting. Although of an almost primitive simplicity, the freshly boiled vegetables make a welcome change from more complicated recipes.

Wash and slice 3 leeks and 2 potatoes, and put them in a saucepan with 1½ pints of cold water. Season with salt and pepper, and bring to the boil. Cook gently till the vegetables are tender and pass through the medium mesh of the food mill. To serve, put a pat of butter in the bottom of each bowl or plate and pour the soup over.

POTAGE PARMENTIER

Fry a medium-sized onion and a small carrot in 1 oz. butter. Add 3 potatoes, a grating of nutmeg and 1½ pints of water. When cooked, pass through a sieve and add a small carton of cream and a handful of coarsely-chopped parsley.

CREAM OF TOMATO

Once you have tasted this delicious soup, you will never again want to eat *any* brand of tinned tomato soup, however little time you have for preparation! I promise you that you can have this soup on the table within 20 minutes of starting to make it.

Fry in butter 4–5 chopped tomatoes, and a medium-sized onion, till soft. Season with salt, pepper, and a pinch of sugar and a pinch of dried basil. Add 2 level tablespoonfuls of concentrated tomato purée and 1½ pints of stock or water. Cook gently till the vegetables are soft enough to pass through a sieve. Dilute a dessertspoonful of cornflour in a teacupful of milk, add to the soup and bring to the boil. Simmer for 2 or 3 minutes and serve with fried croûtons and chopped parsley.

WATERCRESS SOUP

Here is another most refreshing summer soup, which takes next to no time to prepare.

Wash a bunch of watercress and remove the coarse stalks and any yellow leaves. Place the cress in a saucepan with 4 potatoes (about 1 lb.) and 2 pints of water. Season well with salt and pepper and cook gently till the vegetables are tender. Pass through the food mill and just before serving add ½ gill of cream, or top of the milk, and a couple of pats of butter well stirred in.

VICHYSSOISE

This iced soup is really only our old friend Leek and Potato dressed up with the addition of cream and chives. Cut 4 leeks and 4 potatoes into rounds and cook them in 2 pints of water or chicken stock. Season with salt and pepper and when cooked pass through the fine mesh of your food mill. Leave to go cold, and just before serving add a carton of cream and some chopped chives. (If you are unable to get fresh chives, use dried ones, but add them about half-way through the cooking.)

Fish

Prawns and pineapple ✦ Prawn cocktail ✦ Coquilles
St. Jacques Newburg ✦ Scampi à la crème ✦ Moules
poulette ✦ Pilaf de moules ✦ Églefin à l'orange ✦
Flétan à l'américaine ✦ Fish mousse ✦ Fish pie ✦
Fish puffs ✦ Kedgeree ✦ Smoked haddock soufflé
✦ Cold fish with mayonnaise ✦ Pâté of tunny fish ✦
Coquilles au gratin ✦ Salmon cream

Fish

❖❖❖❖❖❖❖❖❖❖❖❖❖❖❖❖❖❖❖❖❖❖❖❖❖❖❖❖❖❖❖❖❖❖❖❖❖❖

PRAWNS AND PINEAPPLE

When prawns are not too expensive you can make a really stunning first course with this recipe.

Allow 2 oz. prawns per person. Fry them gently in butter. When cooked, take them out of the saucepan, while you complete the sauce. Add to your butter the following ingredients per person: a teaspoonful of concentrated tomato purée, 2 tablespoonfuls of cream, and a drop or two of sherry and lemon juice with a suspicion of paprika. Mix well and turn the prawns back into the sauce. Brown in butter some rounds of tinned pineapple (allowing 2–4 per person depending on the size of the pineapple rounds). Arrange the rounds on a dish, place a little heap of prawns over each hole and cover with the sauce, which should be quite thick and not runny. Sprinkle with chopped parsley and serve very hot.

PRAWN COCKTAIL

Again allow 2 oz. prawns per person. For 4 people use a carton of cream, a tablespoonful of white wine, a teaspoonful of vinegar, a dessertspoonful of concentrated tomato purée, a teaspoonful of sugar and a pinch of cayenne pepper. The cream must be fairly stiffly whipped and the other ingredients added gradually, having already been mixed together. Add the prawns last. Serve on a bed of shredded lettuce in glasses, and decorate with slices of lemon and sprigs of parsley.

COQUILLES ST. JACQUES NEWBURG

8 scallops
2 oz. butter
2 tablespoonfuls sherry
2 egg yolks
4 tablespoonfuls rice

Juice of ½ lemon
1 gill cream
1 teaspoonful flour
Salt and cayenne pepper

Clean the scallops well and cut each in half. Fry gently in 1½ oz. butter for 5–7 minutes. Add the juice of half a lemon and cook a minute longer. Add the rest of the butter, and the flour, stirring till it is completely amalgamated. Pour the cream in gradually and bring just to boiling-point. Turn down the heat and add sherry, seasoning, the lightly-beaten egg yolks and the scallops. Heat all together, stirring till the sauce thickens. On no account must it boil or it will curdle. The rice should have been cooked in another saucepan, so that it is ready at the same time as the fish. To serve, arrange the rice in a wall round a circular dish, leaving a hole in the middle which you fill with your scallops and sauce.

SCAMPI À LA CRÈME

Usually made with fresh langoustines—in south-west France the little Dublin Bay prawns are used—but it can be made quite satisfactorily with frozen scampi and a tin of lobster.

Cut the fish in pieces, and cook for a few minutes in butter, seasoning with salt, pepper, paprika and a good teaspoonful of concentrated tomato purée. While this is cooking, beat up the yolks of 2 eggs with a gill of cream. When the pieces of fish are cooked, put in 2 tablespoonfuls of brandy and set it alight. When the flame has died down, combine your cream sauce with your fish mixture, and heat till the sauce is thick. Do not allow it to boil. Serve it as it is or with a dish of plain boiled rice.

MOULES POULETTE

This dish does take rather a long time to prepare on account of the number of times you must wash the mussels. Be careful to pull or scrape off every bit of parasitical matter and, above all, to be sure of removing the beard, a small weed-like thread projecting from the shell. Wash the mussels several times in cold water till no sand or grit remains. In the meantime make a court bouillon of ½ pint of water, a teaspoonful of vinegar, a large wineglass of some dry white wine, a dozen peppercorns, an onion cut up and some parsley stalks. Let this cook for 10–15 minutes. Then put in the mussels, and cover. They are cooked as soon as the shells open. Throw away any which have *not* opened. Keep the mussels warm, still in their shells, and strain the stock. Make a sauce of 1 oz. butter, a teaspoonful of flour, and a pint of the stock. To serve, put the mussels in a deep dish, pour the sauce over and sprinkle liberally with chopped parsley.

PILAF DE MOULES

Prepare the mussels as in the previous recipe, but remove them from their shells and set aside. Make the sauce with the same method as for Moules Poulette, but in the following proportions: 1½ oz. butter, a tablespoonful of flour and 3 pints of stock (from cooking the mussels). Return the mussels to the sauce and add ½ teaspoonful of saffron stirring well in. Cook your rice as recommended on page 17, drain well, arrange in a border and pour the mussels and sauce into the middle.

ÉGLEFIN À L'ORANGE

For 4 people you will need a fresh haddock (or a small hake) weighing 1½–2 lb. To prepare it, put it into a marinade 24 hours before cooking. Lay the fish in a long shallow dish on a bed of thyme, parsley, bay leaves, 2 or 3 small onions stuck with cloves, 2 cloves of garlic, salt and pepper, moistened with a gill of oil. Turn the fish over two or three times during the 24 hours.

The next day put the fish in a well-buttered roasting tin. Moisten with 6 oz. white wine and the juice of an orange. Cook in a moderate oven (Reg. 6) for half an hour, basting occasionally. Take out the fish, drain well and lay it on a serving dish. Keep it warm. Make a sauce with 1 oz. butter, a scant dessertspoonful of flour and the liquid remaining in the roasting tin. Decorate the fish with slices of orange and coarsely-chopped parsley. Strain the sauce and serve in a sauceboat.

FLÉTAN À L'AMÉRICAINE

Have 1½ lb. halibut (or cod) cut into steaks. Roll the steaks in seasoned flour. Heat a tumblerful of oil in a frying-pan and brown the fish. Pour in a tablespoonful of brandy and set alight. When the flames have died down, take out the fish and drain. Keep it warm. Put the liquid from the frying-pan into a saucepan, and add a tumblerful of white wine, 2 tablespoonfuls of tomato purée, salt and pepper, ¼ pint of stock or water, and an onion and a clove of garlic finely chopped. Cover and simmer for half an hour. Put the pieces of fish into the sauce and transfer to a serving dish.

Fish

FISH MOUSSE

¾ lb. salmon, fresh or tinned
2 eggs
½ pint cream

1 dessertspoonful gelatine
dissolved in ⅓ cup of water
Seasoning

Mash the fish thoroughly with a fork, and make sure there are no lumps. Beat in the egg yolks and cook till the mixture thickens, then add the gelatine. Whip the cream stiffly, and thoroughly incorporate it with the mixture. Lastly beat the egg whites to a stiff froth and fold them in carefully. Turn the mousse into a serving dish and put it into the fridge to set. Decorate with slices of lemon.

FISH PIE

When you buy the fish for this dish, make sure your fishmonger gives you the bones and head. Hake or cod is the best, as it flakes easily and holds its consistency. For 4 people allow 1½ lb. without the bones. First make a court bouillon with a pint of cold water, the fish bones, a teaspoonful of vinegar, a glassful of white wine, an onion and a carrot cut up, 2 or 3 cloves, salt, peppercorns, and a bouquet of thyme, parsley and bay leaf. Bring to the boil and cook for 20 minutes, then add the fish and go on cooking gently till tender. In the meantime peel and wash some potatoes and boil in salted water. Lift out the fish, drain, flake and arrange in a dish. Make a sauce with 2 oz. butter, a tablespoonful of flour and a pint of the stock. Sometimes I add a small carton of potted shrimps, which gives additional piquancy, but you must make sure that the spiced butter in which the shrimps are packed is fully melted and amalgamated with your sauce. Pour the sauce over the fish. Strain the potatoes, beat well with a fork to eliminate lumps, and cream with 2 oz. butter and some of the fish stock and/or milk if you have any left. Spread the potato purée over the fish mixture and brown in the oven (Reg. 7 for 10–15 minutes).

This is a most economical dish for large numbers. The extra trouble involved by the making of the court bouillon raises it from the level of a rather insipid and ordinary fish pie to a highly subtle example of culinary skill.

FISH PUFFS

If you have some cooked fish left over, here is a good way to use it up. Mash it in a saucepan with some lemon juice, cream and seasoning, and stir till hot. Have ready some scallop shells or similarly shaped dishes. Arrange some of the fish cream on each shell, then place the yolk of an egg on top. Whip up the whites to stiff peaks, place over the yolks and bake in a hot oven for 5 minutes. This is particularly good when made with smoked haddock.

KEDGEREE

1 smoked haddock weighing 1½ lb.	2 hard-boiled eggs
	Pepper
2 oz. butter	1 teaspoonful concentrated tomato essence
1 gill cream	
A few drops of vinegar	6 tablespoonfuls rice
Lemon juice	

Put the fish in a pan with just enough cold water to cover. Bring slowly to the boil and simmer till cooked. In the meantime cook the rice. Drain the fish and flake it in the saucepan with the butter, tomato purée, lemon juice and vinegar. Mix well, then add, a little at a time so that all is thoroughly combined, the rice and cream. Chop up the hard-boiled eggs, reserve 2 tablespoonfuls and put the rest with the fish. Turn into a dish, sprinkle with the remaining egg and some chopped parsley and serve very hot.

SMOKED HADDOCK SOUFFLÉ

If your guests are prepared to wait, this makes a most attractive first course and you can continue with a cold main dish. It is more satisfactory if made with raw fish, minced, but I have also used cooked haddock with a perfectly good result. You will need 1 lb. smoked haddock fillet, 2 oz. butter, 2 tablespoonfuls of flour, ½ pint of milk, 3 tablespoonfuls of cream and 3 eggs.

Melt the butter in a saucepan and add the flour. Cook, stirring for a few minutes, then add the milk by degrees, continuing to stir until a smooth cream is formed. Put the fish through the mincer if raw, mash with a fork if cooked, and combine with the sauce. When thoroughly mixed, beat in the egg yolks and pass through the medium mesh of the food mill. Whip up the 3 tablespoonfuls of cream, and the egg whites stiffly beaten, and fold into the mixture. Bake about 25 minutes in a hot oven (Reg. 6) and serve immediately.

COLD FISH WITH MAYONNAISE

From the most expensive piece of Scotch salmon to the cheapest cut of cod, the following method of cooking will ensure a most delicate flavour. It makes an ideal main course in hot weather.

Make a court bouillon as in the recipe for *Fish Pie* but ask your fishmonger to give you some additional bones and perhaps a cod's head. A good choice for this dish would be a piece of hake weighing say 1½ lb. Trim off the fins, and cook gently in the court bouillon without removing the central bone. When the fish is almost done, remove the saucepan from the stove and let the fish finish cooking in its own steam. Leave to cool in the court bouillon. To serve, drain, lay on a flat dish and decorate with slices of lemon sprinkled with capers and chopped parsley. Make a thick mayonnaise and serve this in a sauceboat.

Strain the stock and keep it in the fridge. It will make the basis of a good sauce with the remains of your fish.

PÂTÉ OF TUNNY FISH

I often serve this as a first course, accompanied by radishes, black olives and brown bread and butter.

Buy an 8 oz. tin of tunny fish in oil, and turn it into a basin. Mash thoroughly with a fork and add ¼ lb. butter, the juice of half a lemon, 2 tablespoonfuls of olive oil, some freshly-ground pepper and a tablespoonful of brandy. Beat all together till the butter and fish are perfectly mixed, press into a dish and put to set in the fridge. You can either serve it as it is or turn it out on to a plate. Best made the day before.

COQUILLES AU GRATIN

Make a sauce of butter, flour and the remains of a court bouillon. In another saucepan cook in butter an ounce or two of thinly-sliced mushrooms, and add them to the sauce. Flake the remains of some cooked fish and blend into the sauce. Put the mixture in spoonfuls into small individual dishes, cover with breadcrumbs, dot with small pieces of butter and brown in the oven.

Fish

SALMON CREAM

Make this with the excellent imported salmon available at certain times of the year. Cook 1 lb. of the fish in a court bouillon (see page 148) and leave to cool. In the meantime beat the yolks of 3 eggs with a dessertspoonful of flour, turn into a double boiler and add ½ pint of fish stock. Cook till the sauce has thickened and coats the back of a spoon. Pass the fish through the food mill and amalgamate with the sauce. Strain into it a level tablespoonful of gelatine dissolved in a little water. Check seasoning and fold in a cup of whipped cream. Put in the fridge for at least an hour to set.

Meat

Roast pork fillets • Pork spare ribs with barbecue sauce • Roast pork with purée of potatoes • Carré de porc aux pruneaux d'Agen • Jambon aux ananas • Veau à l'estragon • Blanquette de veau (1) & (2) • Veau à la crème • Roast stuffed veal • Rognons de veau au madère • Navarin d'agneau • Roast leg of lamb with rosemary • Rognons d'agneau à la tartare • Ragoût de mouton • Filets de mouton aux marrons • Langues d'agneau farcies • Côtelettes aux concombres • Baked calf's liver • Boeuf paprika • Boeuf à la viennoise • Steak à la portugaise • Queues de boeuf à l'indienne • Daube de boeuf provençale • Spiced salt beef • Boeuf à la mode • Paupiettes de boeuf • Shepherd's pie

Meta

❋❋❋❋❋❋❋❋❋❋❋❋❋❋❋❋❋❋❋❋❋❋❋❋❋❋❋❋❋❋❋❋❋❋❋❋❋❋❋

In most continental countries meat and vegetables are
served as separate courses unless a vegetable is an integral part
of the dish, as for instance in many stews. But generally I
would not recommend including potatoes automatically with
every meat dish you cook. Many of the aromatic stews
cooked with wine are far better with an accompaniment of
pasta—such as spaghetti or noodles—or rice. I have tried in
this chapter to suggest an appropriate accompaniment to each
dish, which can of course be modified. But don't, I beg you,
include potatoes, *however they are cooked*, with any dish containing rice or pasta. You will merely create a starchy stodge.
For all stews with sauce, frankly I would use bread, to mop
up the juice.

ROAST PORK FILLETS

For 4–6 people buy 2 pork fillets weighing about ¾ lb. each.
Split them open lengthwise and lay them on a board. Lay
rashers of unsmoked bacon over the meat and sprinkle with
equal quantities of chopped parsley, thyme and marjoram,
and, sparingly, rosemary. Fold the fillets over and place in a
baking tin. Pour some oil over the meat (about 3 tablespoonfuls per fillet should be enough) and roast for 30–45 minutes
at Reg. 6. The fillets should be brown and crisp on top. To
serve, cut each fillet in slices and arrange on a bed of plain

boiled rice. Pour over them the juices from the tin. The only green vegetable which seems to go with the very aromatic herbs is beans (haricots verts); but I think it is almost better to serve these, or a salad, as a separate course.

PORK SPARE RIBS WITH BARBECUE SAUCE

As you probably know, there isn't a great deal on spare ribs. But as they are extremely cheap you can afford to be generous with your helpings. I usually reckon on 1 side of ribs for 2 people. Cut them into manageable pieces and put them into a baking tin with a little water at the bottom. Cover with a lid or foil and roast for 30 minutes in the oven (Reg. 5). Take them out and pour the liquid away. Then coat each piece of meat with the following sauce:

2 tablespoonfuls concentrated tomato purée	1 tablespoonful marmalade
	1 tablespoonful stock
2 tablespoonfuls ketchup	2 tablespoonfuls oil
1 tablespoonful vinegar	1 very large onion, finely chopped
1 tablespoonful brown sugar	
1 tablespoonful golden syrup	

Heat all together in a saucepan but do not boil.

Put the pieces of coated meat back in the oven and cook for another 30 minutes uncovered. Look at the meat from time to time and baste so that it becomes well browned and glazed.

ROAST PORK WITH PURÉE OF POTATOES

An economical joint to use for this is a hand of pork, which generally is not too fat and is excellent eating when cold. It needs slow cooking—about 30 minutes to the lb. (Reg. 5).

Put a couple of cloves of garlic into the joint and season with salt and a very little rosemary. Put into a baking tin without any fat and cook uncovered, basting frequently. Serve with a purée of potato creamed with the fat and juices from the roast.

CARRÉ DE PORC AUX PRUNEAUX D'AGEN

Agen is the great plum-growing district of France. Most of the fruit is dried and sold as a sweetmeat in jars.

Soak a dozen prunes overnight in ½ pint of claret or burgundy and a tablespoonful of vinegar. Buy a piece of loin of pork and get the butcher to chine it. Divide it into chops and roll each in flour seasoned with salt and a pinch of cinnamon. Sauté the chops in butter until golden. Take them out and keep them warm while you strain the prunes and add to the juices in the pan the wine in which they have soaked. Bring this sauce to the boil stirring all the time so that it is well amalgamated. Replace the chops, and put in the prunes, cover the dish and cook slowly in the oven (Reg. 4) for 30 minutes. The sauce should have thickened, but if it is too runny, reduce it by fiercely boiling for a few moments on the top of the stove. To serve, arrange the chops and prunes in the centre of a serving dish and surround with a border of spring cabbage before pouring the sauce over.

JAMBON AUX ANANAS

You need a piece of ham weighing 3–4 lb. Plug it with 8–10 cloves and put it in a saucepan with cold water to about halfway up. Bring to the boil and cook gently, allowing 25 minutes to the pound. When cooked, remove the cloves and serve hot with fried rings of pineapple and a very creamy purée of potatoes.

Keep the stock—it will form the basis for a wonderful lentil soup (see the recipe on page 28).

VEAU À L'ESTRAGON

Allow a 6 oz. piece of fillet of veal for each person. See that the fillets are well flattened. Roll each piece in flour seasoned with salt, pepper and tarragon, and fry in butter until golden. Take out the fillets and pour into the pan a carton of cream. Stir well so that all the pieces sticking to the bottom and sides of the pan are dislodged. Return the fillets and heat without boiling. Serve immediately.

BLANQUETTE DE VEAU (1)

Veal shrinks quite a lot when stewed, so for 4 people buy 1½–2 lb. You can choose quite a cheap cut, as long as it is lean. Remove any fat and cut the meat into pieces, put in a saucepan and cover with cold water. Add salt and the juice of half a lemon. Bring to the boil and remove the scum. Now add a small glass of dry white wine, a dozen small onions (the kind used for pickling) and a bouquet of parsley, thyme and bay leaf. Cover the saucepan and simmer for about an hour. Strain off the stock and remove the bouquet. Now in another saucepan melt 2 oz. butter and cook 4 oz. mushrooms finely sliced, add a tablespoonful of flour and stir till all is combined. Pour in slowly about ¾ pint of the veal stock. You should now have a creamy sauce. Cook for a further 5 minutes, add a small carton of cream, the meat and a handful of chopped parsley. Heat without boiling and serve in a pre-heated dish.

BLANQUETTE DE VEAU (2)

A simplified version can be made by preparing a sauce with 2 oz. butter, a tablespoonful of flour and ¾ pint of chicken stock. (If you have no stock, use a bouillon cube.) Check seasoning, add the juice of half a lemon and a scrape of nutmeg, put the meat in the sauce, cover the pan and cook for 45–60 minutes. When the veal is cooked, add ½ gill of cream and some chopped parsley, and serve immediately.

VEAU À LA CRÈME

Use good lean veal. Cut 1½ lb. of meat into pieces and fry gently in 1½ oz. butter. When lightly browned, add a small onion finely chopped, cook for 5 minutes and season with salt and pepper. Pour away the remaining fat and add a gill of double cream and 2 tablespoonfuls of white stock. Mix well, then stir in a tablespoonful of concentrated tomato purée, and paprika pepper to taste. The flavour of this last should be quite strong. Heat without boiling. Serve with steamed new potatoes and a plain green salad.

ROAST STUFFED VEAL

Make a stuffing of breadcrumbs, thyme, grated lemon peel and chopped streaky bacon and bind with a little boiling water and the yolk of an egg. Buy a piece of rolled and boned veal and lard it all over with the stuffing. Roast it slowly (Reg. 5) allowing 25 minutes to the pound. Serve with a jardinière of new peas and young whole carrots plainly boiled, well drained, and tossed in butter. This makes a lovely main course for a spring dinner party.

ROGNONS DE VEAU AU MADÈRE

A veal kidney should be enough for 2 people. Remove all fat and skin, and slice thinly. Fry gently in butter and when half cooked add 2 tablespoonfuls of madeira or sherry. (In the latter case put a couple of lumps of sugar into the sauce.) Let the sauce bubble for a minute or two then lower the heat and finish the cooking at a merest simmer. Serve with a purée of green peas, and add a little of the water in which they were cooked to thin the sauce.

NAVARIN D'AGNEAU

The best cuts to use for this are either slices of shoulder or loin chops. Allow approximately 6 oz. per person. Remove fat. Melt 2 oz. butter in a frying-pan with a heaped teaspoonful of caster sugar. Brown the meat, then take it out of the pan and roll it in seasoned flour. When thoroughly coated, put back into the pan and allow to brown again. Add 3–4 tomatoes, peeled and chopped, a bouquet of parsley, thyme and bay leaf, and enough stock or water to just cover the meat. Transfer all to a casserole and cook, covered, in a slow oven (Reg. 3) for an hour. Meanwhile boil 1 lb. new peas, a young turnip thinly sliced and some new carrots and potatoes. The carrots and potatoes can be cooked in the same saucepan together. Drain the vegetables well, add them at the end of the hour to the meat, and return to the oven for a further 15 minutes. Remove the bouquet, check seasoning, and if the sauce seems too thick add a little of the water you cooked the peas in.

One word of warning. To make sure your sauce isn't too greasy, pour away any surplus fat from the frying-pan before adding the tomatoes and the water or stock.

ROAST LEG OF LAMB WITH ROSEMARY

Insert a clove of garlic just above the bone, rub the joint with salt and sprinkle with rosemary. Place a good piece of dripping in the pan and roast in the usual way, basting frequently. Serve with basil potatoes (see page 99.)

ROGNONS D'AGNEAU À LA TARTARE

Allow 2 kidneys per person. Skin and split the kidneys and cook them in butter. Place on squares of fried bread and fill the centres with a spoonful of very thick tartare sauce (see page 146.) Serve with watercress.

RAGOÛT DE MOUTON

You can use a cheap cut of meat for this stew. Neck or loin are good bets, but make sure it is not too fat. In any case, take off as much fat as you can. In an earthenware casserole spread a layer of sliced potatoes, then a layer of thickly sliced onions, then the meat. Before covering with another layer of onions and lastly potatoes, insert a bouquet of parsley stalks, thyme and bay leaves. Season and add half white wine and half stock to come half-way up the sides of the casserole. Cover and cook slowly for $1\frac{1}{2}$–2 hours in a slow oven (Reg. 3).

FILETS DE MOUTON AUX MARRONS

Get the butcher to bone a loin of lamb for you and cut it in slices, removing any fat. Roll them in beaten egg and breadcrumbs and fry in very hot oil. At the same time, in another pan, grill some chipolata sausages. Serve with braised chestnuts and celery.

To prepare the chestnuts, which can be done the day before, make a slit in the side of each nut, and put in a moderate oven for about 10 minutes, when you should easily be able to remove the outer shell. Boil the chestnuts in salted water for 20 minutes, drain, and remove the inner skin. When required, cook them in water or stock for another 10 minutes, drain, and return to the pan with an ounce of butter. Toss them carefully so that they become well coated and brown.

LANGUES D'AGNEAU FARCIES

These small tongues can be rather insipid when plainly boiled, but the following recipe will give you a most unusual dish and a welcome change.

Boil the tongues in salted water till they are tender enough to remove the skins. Split them down the middle and lay them in a shallow dish. Now chop together ¼ lb. mushrooms, ¼ lb. ham, ¼ lb. shallots; add 2 tablespoonfuls of chopped parsley, 2 tablespoonfuls of soft breadcrumbs, the juice of half a lemon and a grating of lemon peel. Bind with the yolk of an egg and 2 oz. butter. Beat well together and spread the mixture over each half tongue. Bake in a medium oven (Reg. 5) till brown (about 20 minutes). Serve with sauté potatoes.

CÔTELETTES AUX CONCOMBRES

When you are really in a hurry and have no time for cooking a joint, try this unfamiliar combination. Season your cutlets and grill. Serve with cucumber cut into cubes and lightly fried in butter.

BAKED CALF'S LIVER

Arrange in an oblong dish some slices of liver, with between each one a thick rasher of bacon, a thick slice of onion and a bay leaf. Season, but be sparing with the salt on account of the bacon. Put a little stock at the bottom of the dish and dot with small pieces of butter. Cover with a buttered paper before putting on a lid, or hermetically sealing with foil. Bake for 30 minutes (Reg. 5) and serve with plain boiled rice and a green salad.

BOEUF PAPRIKA

For 4 people you will need 1½ lb. lean beef, preferably a piece of top rump. Cut it in slices, and fry gently in butter. Add a medium-sized chopped onion and let it and the meat cook till golden. Season with salt and pepper, and stir. Now pour off the superfluous fat and add a good tablespoonful of tomato purée and enough, approximately ½ teaspoonful, paprika to give the dish its very individual flavour. Remove from the heat and mix in a large carton of cream (⅓ pint). Return to the stove, turn down the heat, cover and let simmer very slowly till the meat is cooked—about half an hour. Serve with plain boiled new potatoes liberally sprinkled with parsley.

BOEUF À LA VIENNOISE

The flavour of caraway seeds doesn't appeal to everybody, so find out first if your guests are allergic to the taste of aniseed before you embark on this unusual beef stew.

Use 1½ lb. of lean beef as in the previous recipe. Melt an ounce of butter in a frying-pan and brown a chopped onion. Add the meat, cut into large cubes and well seasoned with salt and pepper, and cook over a slowish heat for about 10 minutes. Sprinkle a dessertspoonful of flour and stir well, then add by degrees a gill of stock or water, and 2 tablespoonfuls of sherry. Tie a teaspoonful of caraway seeds in a piece of thin muslin, and bury this in the centre of the meat. Cover and leave to cook slowly. In another pan melt 4 rashers of bacon cut in $\frac{1}{2}$-in. strips. Remove the caraway seeds, and add the bacon and cook for a further 5 minutes. Serve with a hot salad of apples, sliced and fried without sugar, in butter. You will get the best results by using a good crisp dessert apple.

STEAK À LA PORTUGAISE

Buy rump steak for this and get your butcher to cut as large slices as possible. Roll the meat in flour and fry in a mixture of butter and oil over a fierce fire to seal the juices. Then add 2 tablespoonfuls of brandy and set alight. When the flame has died down, add seasoning and a little stock or water and continue to cook gently till the meat is tender. It should not take more than 5–7 minutes. In the meantime thinly slice 2 oz. mushrooms and put them into the sauce. Just before serving pour in 2 tablespoonfuls of cream. Bring to the boil, stirring well, arrange in a serving dish and sprinkle with parsley.

QUEUES DE BOEUF À L'INDIENNE

Ox-tail cooked in a spicy curry sauce makes a good change from the usual brown gravy of indeterminate origin and tired vegetables. Ox-tail takes a long time to become tender and is very fat, so cook it the day before it is required so that you can easily remove all the excess fat from the stock before you make the sauce. For 4 people buy 2 ox-tails, and get the butcher to cut them into pieces. Soak them for an hour or two in cold salted water and then drain them. (You can do this a further day in advance and it will keep perfectly well in the fridge.) Cut up 4 rashers of unsmoked bacon into cubes and heat them with 2 oz. butter in a heavy frying-pan. Now fry a large sliced onion till golden brown. Add the meat, and fry it quickly and transfer it to a casserole (unless you have one of the flame-proof casseroles which you can use for the whole operation). Pour ½ pint of water into the frying-pan and stir well. Season with salt and pepper and a bouquet of parsley, thyme and bay leaf. Add to the meat in the casserole and cover and cook in a slow oven (Reg. 3) for 2–3 hours. Leave to go cold, when the fat can be easily removed.

On the day the dish is required, make a sauce with an ounce of butter, a dessertspoonful of flour, a teaspoonful of tomato purée, a teaspoonful of curry powder, and the unstrained liquid from the meat. Stir well till the flour is cooked, then pour the sauce over the ox-tails and cook in the oven for half an hour when the meat should be almost falling off the bones. Serve with boiled rice.

DAUBE DE BOEUF PROVENÇALE

A daubière is an earthenware casserole used for braising meat. A daube is usually of beef well larded with salt pork. This particular stew, which is almost more delectable warmed up the day after it is made, is cooked with wine and is characterized by the very strong flavour of tomatoes. Fry an onion in 2 tablespoonfuls of oil till golden. Roll your meat (1½ lb. lean stewing steak—shin does very well) in salt and a little marjoram or oregano, brown quickly and remove to a plate while you heat ¼ lb. unsmoked bacon chopped into cubes. Now add a glass of red wine (about 6 fluid oz.) and let it bubble. Stir in 2 tablespoonfuls of tomato purée and a clove of garlic and mix well. Return the meat to the casserole and add enough water to cover. Check the seasoning and cover tightly. Cook for at least 2½ hours in a slow oven (Reg. 2), by which time the meat should be tender and the sauce reduced and thickened. Serve in the casserole accompanied by a dish of spaghetti, boiled and lightly tossed in butter or oil. A plain green salad can be offered as a separate vegetable.

SPICED SALT BEEF

Buy 2 lb. salt brisket in one piece and put it in a saucepan of cold water. Bring to the boil and throw the water away. Now put into the pan 2 carrots cut into large pieces, an onion, 12 peppercorns and a bunch of herbs (parsley, thyme and bay leaf). Rub the meat in a teaspoonful of ground cloves mixed with a teaspoonful of ground mace or nutmeg, and lay it on the vegetables. Add water just to cover, put on the lid and simmer gently for about 3 hours. Equally good hot or cold.

BOEUF À LA MODE

Here is another of those dishes which taste equally good hot or cold. Lard a piece of beef (topside or top rump), weighing about 2 lb., with pieces of pork fat. Brown in some good dripping. Take it out of the pan and fry a couple of onions. Now pour in 2 tablespoonfuls of brandy and set alight. When the flames have died down, add a large glass of red wine and let it bubble. Add 2 carrots, a bouquet of herbs (parsley, thyme and bay leaf) a calf's foot if you can get it, otherwise 2 pig's trotters, and a clove of garlic. Lay the meat on the vegetables and pour in enough stock or water to cover. Put on the lid and simmer on the lowest possible heat for at least 3 hours. When done, take out the meat (it should be quite soft, but will firm up when cold), put in a dish, and strain the stock over. Leave to cool and then put in the fridge for several

hours. When it is completely chilled, you will be able to remove all the fat and you will be left with a clear, not too stiff,
jelly. Serve with a green salad and no potatoes.

PAUPIETTES DE BOEUF

Get your butcher to cut a piece of top rump into slices, about
¼ in. thick. Allow a rasher of streaky bacon for each slice and
chop it finely. Make a stuffing of an ounce of bread soaked in
a tablespoonful of hot milk, the chopped bacon, a heaped
tablespoonful of chopped parsley, and a medium-sized
onion, together with ¼ lb. mushrooms chopped and previously cooked in an ounce of butter. Mix well, and lay a
spoonful of the stuffing on each slice of meat. Roll up and tie
with strong cotton or fine string. Brown the rolls in a frying-
pan in another ounce of butter, then lay them in a casserole
and moisten with a gill of stock. Cover and simmer for an
hour and a half, then remove the string and arrange the meat
on a dish. Stir the sauce well in order to detach all the par-
ticles adhering to the sides of the pan (if necessary add a little
more stock), heat thoroughly and strain on to the meat.

SHEPHERD'S PIE

This is an excellent way of using up the remains of a joint.

Mince the meat. In a saucepan melt an ounce of dripping
and fry a large chopped onion. Stir in a teaspoonful of flour,
half a glass of white wine and a breakfast cup of cold water.
Mix well, then add the minced meat, a tablespoonful of
tomato purée, salt and plenty of freshly-milled pepper, and
allow to simmer, stirring from time to time. Meanwhile boil
some potatoes (for 4 people, 1½ lb), put them through the
food mill and return to the saucepan with a good lump of

butter and ½ pint of either milk or bouillon. Beat well so that you get a creamy purée. Pour the meat mixture into a deepish dish, cover completely with the potato purée and brown in a hot oven for 8–10 minutes.

Poultry and Game

Roast chicken • Chicken à la chinoise • Chicken à l'américaine • Poulet en cocotte Landaise • Chicken à la crème • Poulet sauté au vin blanc • Poulet sauté Girondin • Poulet Saint Valentin • Canard Verjus • Roast duck à l'orange • Canard aux olives Joyeux • Braised pheasant • Roast pheasant with braised celery • Stewed pigeons • Partridges in vine leaves • Perdreaux Charentais • Lapin à la niçoise • Lapin aux pruneaux

Poultry and Game

❖❖

Although it is rare in these days to buy a chicken which has not been drawn and cleaned, it does sometimes happen that one buys from a farm, or maybe a country market, a bird which is plucked and singed, but otherwise unprepared for cooking. As I once spent a highly mysterious and baffling half-hour groping about in the inside of a bird wondering why I could not find the intestines, which I had been told would emerge almost in one piece, I thought it might be useful to begin this chapter with a simple instruction on how to draw a chicken, turkey or duck. In cooking game birds the intestines are left in, except for pheasant, which is drawn like a chicken.

Put the bird on the table and cut off the claws and the legs up to the first joint. Then remove the head as far up the neck as possible. Now turn the bird round. With the point of a sharp knife make a slit just above the tail, where there is already a small hole. With a piece of clean rag put your hand into the body of the bird and draw out the intestines. Keep the gizzard, the liver and the heart and throw the rest away. Make an incision round the top of the gizzard, taking care not to pierce the bag inside, which contains undigested food. This you also throw away. Cut off the little green bag attached to the liver, which holds the gall. This is very important, as it will give a bitter taste to your bird if left. Wash the bird and the giblets in water, drain well and put on a plate till required.

In a duck, on each side of the rump (parson's nose) there are two glands which you must take care to remove, as if left in they can give an unpleasant taste.

ROAST CHICKEN

I must admit that, generally speaking, the French roast a chicken better than any other nationality. The secret, of course, is in the amount of butter put inside the bird and the frequent basting. The result is a bird cooked to a moisture and delicacy obtained by no other means, though an excellent imitation can be obtained, if you have no time to baste, by hermetically sealing the bird in foil.

For a chicken for 4 people rub the outside with the juice of half a lemon and add a good spreading of butter. Fill the inside with a piece of butter weighing about $\frac{1}{4}$ lb., the liver and a half lemon. Wrap in foil and cook in a hot oven (Reg. 7) allowing 25 minutes to the pound. Remove the foil for the last 10 minutes. Place the bird on a dish and keep it warm in the oven having emptied the juices out of it into the roasting pan. Now pour in a little stock which you have made from the giblets. Serve this sauce separately and put the chicken on a serving dish, with plenty of watercress.

CHICKEN À LA CHINOISE

Crush a clove of garlic with a teaspoonful of sugar and a tea-spoonful of coriander seeds, previously roasted for 2–3 minutes in the oven, and work into a sauce with 2 tablespoon-fuls of soya sauce, a tablespoonful of oil, salt and freshly-ground black pepper. Rub the sauce thoroughly into the chicken and leave for 15 minutes. Roast in the ordinary way, and serve with boiled rice, mixed with a cup of diced cooked pork and some pineapple rings and lettuce all lightly fried in oil.

CHICKEN À L'AMÉRICAINE

I found this version of chicken Maryland quite delicious, and it is easily and quickly prepared.

Divide a small roasting chicken into four, and brush with oil. Roll in flour lightly seasoned with salt and pepper. Fry 4 rashers of fairly fat bacon, then add the chicken joints and cook till brown. Add half a teacupful of cream and continue cooking uncovered for about 5 minutes when the cream should have thickened. Now add another half-cupful of cream, cover and simmer gently for a further 15 minutes. During this time slice some bananas lengthwise and fry till brown. Arrange the chicken in the centre of a dish and place the bananas all round it with some spoonfuls of heated sweet corn. Pour the cream sauce over it, sprinkle with parsley and serve quickly.

POULET EN COCOTTE LANDAISE

This is an ideal way to cook a chicken when either you have guests who are likely to be late, or you yourself want to find something ready if you have been out in the early part of the evening. You can prepare the whole thing the day before and heat it up in next to no time.

For 4 people you will need 4 chicken joints, or a bird cut into quarters. First soak a dozen prunes in $\frac{1}{2}$ pint of red wine and a tablespoonful of wine vinegar, allowing 3 hours. When you are ready to prepare your cocotte, chop 2 onions with a clove of garlic and lightly brown them in 2 oz. butter. Now brown the pieces of chicken, and when well coloured take them out and put them on a warm plate. Remove the prunes from the wine, drain well, and roll each one in a rasher of streaky bacon. Sauté them over a moderate heat for about 10 minutes, then pour in the wine and vinegar, check the seasoning, add the chicken and its juices, and a large green pepper cut into narrow strips. (Make sure you cut off the end of the pepper and remove all the seeds, as they are very bitter. The best way to do this is to hold the pepper under the cold tap for a moment or two, so that all the stray seeds get washed away.) Cover the casserole and put it in a slow oven (Reg. 3) for an hour. Serve with boiled rice and a green salad.

CHICKEN À LA CRÈME

For this you will need a boiling fowl. Peel 2 carrots and an onion and prepare a bouquet of herbs, salt and pepper. Put these, together with the chicken, into a saucepan of cold water—enough just to cover the top of the breast bone. Bring to the boil, lower the heat and let simmer. It will take at least 2 hours, or, if a very old bird, even longer. When it is really tender, take it out and put it on a plate. In another saucepan melt 2 oz. butter, add ¼ lb. thinly-sliced mushrooms, with a teaspoonful of chopped tarragon, and cook gently till soft. Then sprinkle into the pan a dessertspoonful of flour, stir well with a wooden spoon and pour in, away from the fire, enough of the strained stock to make a thinnish creamy sauce. Return to the heat, bring to the boil, cook gently for a further 5 minutes, stirring all the time, then add a small carton of cream. Carve the chicken into convenient sized pieces, arrange in a dish and pour the sauce over. This is particularly delicious served with *petits pois à la française* (see page 108).

POULET SAUTÉ AU VIN BLANC

Divide a chicken into four and remove the skin. Melt an ounce of butter in a flame-proof casserole and cook an onion, cut into thin rings, for a few minutes. It must not be darker than pale gold. Remove it and set aside. Add 2 oz. more butter to the casserole and gently fry the pieces of chicken, taking care not to let them brown. Cook for about 10 minutes turning the pieces from time to time. Now return the onion to the casserole, add the giblets, cover and put into a hot oven (Reg. 6) for 10–12 minutes. While the chicken is in the oven, make a Béchamel with 1 oz. flour, 1 oz. butter and ½ pint of milk. Season with salt and pepper. Cook gently for a minute or two then add the onion from the casserole. Remove the giblets from the casserole and discard. Keep the pieces of chicken warm. Now add 2 tablespoonfuls of cognac to the Béchamel and set alight. When the flame has subsided reduce the sauce a little, strain it into a clean saucepan and add a small pat of butter, the juice of half a lemon and 4 oz. white wine. Reheat the sauce and coat the pieces of chicken. Sprinkle with parsley before serving.

POULET SAUTÉ GIRONDIN

In certain parts of the Gironde (the south-west department of France of which Bordeaux is the capital), chestnut trees grow in great profusion, and I first met this unusual way of cooking chicken in a tiny restaurant near La Réole (one of Henry II's last strongholds in France).

Cut up a roasting chicken into joints and season with salt and pepper. Melt an ounce of butter in a heavy pan, and fry 4 oz. fat pork (belly is the best for this), cut into cubes. When it is beginning to colour, add the pieces of chicken and cook to a light brown. Pour off any surplus fat and add a bouquet of herbs and a small glass of sherry. In the little restaurant they used madeira, but I have had quite good results with vermouth or sherry. Cover the pan and cook fairly quickly for 5 minutes. Reduce the heat and continue cooking gently until the meat is tender. In another saucepan heat some chestnut purée, which you have made according to the recipe for *Filets de mouton aux marrons* (page 54). Beat in a good pat of butter, and arrange in a wall round a circular dish. Put the pieces of chicken in the middle, pour the pan juices over, and serve with croûtons fried crisp in very hot oil.

POULET SAINT VALENTIN

When I was a young girl I used to stay with some great friends who had an estate between Salzburg and Linz (the birthplace of Mozart). The Schloss had been a medieval convent and my chief recollection is of the fantastically tiled roof with hundreds of white pigeons perched on the crenellations as if they were part of the decoration.

The cook, who was a native of the village, used to prepare chickens from this recipe, which she declared had been handed down through generations of her forebears.

Cut a roasting chicken into neat joints and brown them on both sides in 2 oz. butter. Season with a little paprika, salt and nutmeg. Pour away half the fat, sprinkle a tablespoonful of flour on the chicken joints. Stir well and add a wineglass of white wine and ½ pint of milk. Bring to the boil, still stirring, then turn down the heat, cover and simmer for half an hour. While the chicken is cooking, put 4 tablespoonfuls of rice in another saucepan with a pint of white stock, if possible (otherwise use water), flavoured with paprika, salt and nutmeg. When cooked, the rice should have absorbed all the stock, but if any remains, boil fiercely till evaporated. Now mix in 2 oz. chopped ham, a handful of chopped parsley and 2 oz. butter. Arrange the chicken joints in the centre of a dish, with the rice as a border. Add the juice of half a lemon to the sauce, reduce by letting it boil fiercely for a minute or two, stir in a pat of butter, and strain over the chicken. A plain green salad is the only accompaniment you need.

CANARD VERJUS

Verjus is a term used in wine growing districts to denote acid, or unripe grapes. For this very piquant recipe for cooking duck, use the small green South African grapes which are very cheap in the summer months. For a medium-sized duck you will need ½ lb. of grapes, which you must blanch to soften the skins.

Roast the duck in a covered pan, and while it is cooking prepare the following sauce. Cut 4 rashers of streaky bacon into dice and heat them in an ounce of butter. Add 2 medium-sized carrots, or 1 large one, chopped, a small onion also chopped, a bouquet of parsley, thyme and bay leaf, and salt and pepper. When browned, sprinkle a tablespoonful of flour and mix well. Add a wineglass (4 oz.) of white wine and a pint of meat stock. (If you have no stock, use a good make of bouillon cube.) Bring to the boil, stirring well, and allow to re-duce a little, then cover, and cook for half an hour. Pass through the fine mesh of the food mill, add 2 medium-sized tomatoes, cook for 15 minutes and pass again through the strainer. Add the grapes and a good tablespoonful of redcurrant jelly. The sauce should now be of a creamy consistency, but if it still seems too thin reduce it a little, and then let it simmer till you are ready to use it. The grapes should be just soft.

ROAST DUCK À L'ORANGE

A duck is a very fat bird, so put it in a pan with a little water and no other fat. After roasting it uncovered for half an hour (Reg.5), pour the fat away, and put it back into the oven with a little more water and the giblets. Cook for another half an hour, or longer, basting frequently. When it is done, take it out, keep it warm and add to the juices in the pan the juice of an orange and the rind of half an orange cut into match-sized strips. Cook on the top of the stove till the rinds are soft. Now sprinkle a tablespoonful of flour, let it cook for a few minutes, then add enough stock to make the sauce of a creamy consistency. Carve the duck, and serve with *Petits pois à la Française* (see page 108). The sauce should accompany it in a sauceboat.

CANARD AUX OLIVES JOYEUX

One of the most imaginative cooks I ever met was our *régisseur*, and his way of cooking duck with olives was in the class of great cookery. Here is his recipe.

To make the stuffing, stone and chop 24 green olives and combine with 2 oz. bread soaked in water and squeezed dry, 2 oz. chopped mushrooms, ½ a clove of garlic minced, the liver of the duck, a tablespoonful of minced parsley and a little pepper. Bind with a beaten egg. Stuff the bird, and either sew it up, or make sure the flap of skin is well tucked under to prevent the stuffing escaping. Roast in the ordinary way, basting frequently and pouring away some of the fat. When the bird is half cooked, put another dozen olives into the roasting pan. To serve, cut the duck into convenient pieces with some of the stuffing on each one, leave a little fat in the pan, pour away the rest and add a little stock which you have made from the giblets (neck, gizzard and heart). Pour this over the pieces of duck, and serve with plain boiled new potatoes, well coated with chopped parsley.

BRAISED PHEASANT

This is a marvellous way of cooking a tough old bird, as the slow stewing not only brings out the flavour but guarantees absolute tenderness of the meat.

Roll the pheasant in seasoned flour, brown in butter and when well coloured remove from the pan and fry half a dozen rashers of streaky bacon in the same fat. Now blanch a young cabbage in boiling salted water, drain it well, cut away the hard stalky parts and separate the leaves. Carve the bird. In a casserole put a layer of the cabbage leaves, then the pieces of pheasant, 4 frankfurter sausages and a bouquet of parsley, thyme and bay leaf. Cover with the remaining cabbage leaves. Pour a good teacupful of stock or water into the frying-pan, stir well to amalgamate the juices and pour it over the meat and cabbage. Cover the casserole with a lid or foil and cook in a slow oven (Reg. 3) for 2–3 hours.

This dish takes very kindly to re-heating and so you can make it the day before you need it. It is also good with stewing partridges, but add a piece of orange peel to the bouquet, which must be removed before serving.

ROAST PHEASANT WITH BRAISED CELERY

Cover the pheasant with rashers of fat bacon and tie well. As pheasant is inclined to be rather dry, put a lump of butter inside the bird. Grate some lemon rind over and wrap up in foil. Roast (Reg. 6) for 40–45 minutes. Serve with braised celery.

Poultry and Game

STEWED PIGEONS

Allow 1 pigeon per person. Brown them all over in butter, then take them out and cook in the same butter an onion and a carrot chopped. When these are becoming soft and brown, sprinkle with a tablespoonful of flour and stir well. Add a small wineglassful of red wine, a tablespoonful of tomato purée, a bouquet of herbs and enough stock to make a creamy sauce. Put the pigeons into a casserole and pour the sauce over. Cook in a slow oven (Reg. 4). If the birds are young, half an hour should be long enough, but if you buy them as stewing pigeons, they will need at least an hour. In the meantime fry 2 or 3 rashers of bacon chopped into cubes and some tiny onions (the kind for pickling) to which you have added a teaspoonful of sugar. If you can get hold of some cranberries, make a compôte with 1 lb. cranberries stewed without sugar in a teacupful of water. When cooked, press the fruit against the sides of the saucepan to release the juice and stir in 2 or 3 tablespoonfuls of sugar (more if you have a very sweet tooth!). Add the bacon and onions to the sauce with the pigeons and transfer the cranberry compôte to a glass dish.

PARTRIDGES IN VINE LEAVES

Tie a slice of fat pork and a piece of lemon peel over the breast of each partridge and put a lump of butter inside. Wrap each bird in vine leaves. If you are unable to get fresh ones, you can buy tins containing about half a pound, and the leaves will keep quite well in the fridge for several days. Put the partridges in a covered dish and roast in a fairly hot oven (Reg. 6) for 30–45 minutes.

PERDREAUX CHARENTAIS

Our milk used to be supplied by a native of the great dairy-producing part of the Charente—the other part is famous for the grapes which provide the basis of the great brandies. Madame Muret was a famous cook in our village and was flattered rather than otherwise when one begged for the secret of one of her specialities. I found the following way of serving old partridges quite delicious.

Season the birds with salt, pepper and lemon juice, brown all over in butter, add enough stock or water to half cover the birds, and stew gently on top of the stove or in the oven for an hour and a half. While the partridges are cooking, make a compôte of apples flavoured with a little brown sugar. Spread the compôte on a dish and when the birds are cooked, halve them, lay them on the apple, cover each half with a tablespoonful of cream, put them in a hot oven for a few minutes and then serve immediately.

LAPIN À LA NIÇOISE

Cut the rabbit into pieces and roll in seasoned flour. Heat 3 tablespoonfuls of oil in a frying-pan and fry the pieces of rabbit till golden. Pour in a glass of white wine and let it bubble for a minute or two. Add about 15 black olives, ½ lb. tomatoes slightly cooked without water and passed through a sieve, and a bouquet of parsley, thyme and bay leaf. Cover and cook very gently for 25 minutes. Take out the pieces of meat and arrange them on a dish and keep them warm while you add to the sauce 2 oz. butter. Mix well, pour the sauce over the meat and serve at once.

LAPIN AUX PRUNEAUX

This classic method of cooking rabbit is also excellent with chicken.

Wash some prunes and leave them to soak overnight. Cut the rabbit in pieces and place them in a casserole. Pour over them a heated marinade made with a large carrot cut in rounds, half a bottle of red wine, a wineglassful of water and a bouquet of parsley, thyme and bay leaf. Leave also to soak overnight, making sure that all the pieces of rabbit are covered with the marinade.

The next day melt $1\frac{1}{2}$ oz. butter in a pan and brown 2 medium-sized onions, sliced, and $\frac{1}{4}$ lb. fat bacon chopped into little cubes. Add the pieces of rabbit from the marinade and brown well. Strain the marinade over the meat, season with salt and pepper and add the drained prunes. Transfer to a casserole, cover and cook in a slow oven (Reg. 4) for an hour. Serve as it is, accompanied by a green vegetable (young cabbage is particularly good). If the sauce is too thin, reduce by boiling for a minute or two.

Supper Dishes

Crêpes Florentine • Crêpes aux épinards Mornay •
Crêpes au Gryère • Crêpes aux champignons •
Fondue Franc-Comtoise • Tartines Marquise •
Beignets de fromage blanc • Croquettes au fromage
• Croustades au Gruyère • Gougère • Stuffed cab-
bage • Veal and ham cheese • Mexican rolls •
Spaghetti bolognese • Laitues de la Mère Lan-
durette • Pilaf à la reine • Pork with Jambalaya rice
• Gâteau de volaille à la crème

Supper Dishes

CRÊPES

There is a restaurant in Paris which serves only pancakes, and until one has eaten the many original and delectable fillings, one does not realize how attractive a meal can be produced with the minimum of expense. The preparation is really not such a complicated affair as it might appear.

First, your batter. To make 12–14 pancakes, put 8 rounded tablespoonfuls of flour into a basin with a teaspoonful of salt. Now stir in 2 tablespoonfuls of oil and 2 whole eggs. When this is well mixed add ½ pint of milk and cold water in equal quantities. Stir again until there are no lumps, and strain into a clean basin. Cover and leave to stand for at least 2 hours. When you are ready to cook the pancakes, run a few drops of oil over the bottom of a frying-pan and, with a ladle or large spoon, quickly pour in a thin layer of batter. Allow to cook for a moment or two, move the pan till the whole of the surface is covered with the batter, then with a palette knife turn the pancake over and fry the other side. The whole operation should take no more than a minute for each pancake. Lay the pancakes one on top of the other on a plate till wanted.

CRÊPES FLORENTINE

Cook 1 lb. spinach, squeeze out the water and put it through the food mill. Now put it in the top of a double

77

saucepan, with 2 or 3 tablespoonfuls of cream, the same amount of stock and the yolks of 2 eggs. Season with salt, pepper, a scrape of nutmeg and a pinch of sugar. Stir till the mixture thickens. Spread out the required number of pancakes and lay a good spoonful of the spinach mixture on each one. Roll up, lay side by side in a dish, cover and keep warm till wanted. Serve with a basil-flavoured tomato sauce.

CRÊPES AUX ÉPINARDS MORNAY

Prepare the spinach as in the previous recipe, but when drained and sieved mix it with a cheese-flavoured Béchamel (for the basic method see page 142), spiced with a little nutmeg. Fill the pancakes as before and serve without the addition of any other sauce.

CRÊPES AU GRUYÈRE

Make a very thick Béchamel with 1½ oz. butter, 2 tablespoonfuls of flour and a pint of milk, seasoned with nutmeg, salt and pepper. When thoroughly amalgamated, add 2 oz. grated gruyère, cheddar or parmesan. Fill the pancakes with the sauce, roll them up and arrange in a fireproof dish. Sprinkle with grated cheese and slivers of almonds. Put in a hot oven to brown for about 10 minutes.

CRÊPES AUX CHAMPIGNONS

Fry a medium-sized onion, chopped finely, in 1½ oz. butter. Add 6 oz. mushrooms, thinly sliced, and 2 oz. chopped bacon or ham. When the mushrooms are cooked, sprinkle a tablespoonful of flour into the pan, stir well and add gradually ½ pint of stock. If you have some stock from chicken bones, so much the better. Cook a little longer, fill the pancakes as before, sprinkle liberally with chopped parsley and serve at once.

FONDUE FRANC-COMTOISE

This is a French regional variation of a Swiss fondue, made with light local wine. It has the merit of very quick preparation.

Rub the bottom of a fireproof dish with a crushed clove of garlic. Pour in a gill of white wine and warm it. Now add 2 tablespoonfuls of grated gruyère and cook it gently, stirring frequently, till the sauce becomes creamy. Beat up 6 eggs as if you were going to make an omelette and stir them into the cheese sauce, together with 2 oz. butter. Allow to simmer for 7–8 minutes, while the mixture thickens, season with salt, pepper and a good pinch of grated nutmeg, and serve in a well buttered and heated dish, with fingers of toast.

TARTINES MARQUISE

Make a Béchamel with $1\frac{1}{2}$ oz. butter, $1\frac{1}{2}$ tablespoonfuls of flour and $\frac{1}{2}$ pint milk. When smooth and creamy, stir in the yolks of 2 eggs and 4 tablespoonfuls of grated cheese. Cut the required number of slices of bread and cover them thickly with the sauce. Have ready a frying-pan half full of oil, heat it up to boiling-point (there should be the faintest suspicion of smoke rising from the pan). Slip the tartines into the boiling fat and fry till golden. Serve immediately.

BEIGNETS DE FROMAGE BLANC

Boil 1 lb. potatoes till soft and pass them through a sieve. Beat into them a whole egg, $\frac{1}{2}$ lb. cottage cheese, sieved, salt and pepper, the grated rind of a lemon and 3 tablespoonfuls of flour. Mix together, flour your hands and roll the mixture into little sausage-like shapes. Fry these in very hot oil and drain on soft paper. Serve at once.

CROQUETTES AU FROMAGE

Make a thick Béchamel with 2½ oz. butter, 3 tablespoonfuls of flour and a pint of milk. Season with salt and pepper and stir in the yolks of 2 eggs and 5 tablespoonfuls of grated cheese. Roll the paste into thumb-sized sausages and fry in very hot fat. Drain on paper and serve with bunches of parsley.

CROUSTADES AU GRUYÈRE

In a double saucepan cook ½ cup of milk, 4 tablespoonfuls of grated cheese, 2 oz. butter, a whole egg, salt, pepper and a scrape of nutmeg. Stir till the mixture has sufficiently thickened (it should be almost solid) to spread on pieces of buttered toast. Brown quickly under the grill and serve at once.

GOUGÈRE

We had a manservant whose home was near Vezelay, one of the most beautiful centres of Roman civilization in France. Like all Burgundians, he was a great cheese eater, and particularly fond of cooked-cheese dishes. The following recipe, for which our cook used to hand over her kitchen to him, is the most famous cheese dish of Burgundy, and I give it with the instructions as written for me when I got married.

'Make a pâte à choux with 3 oz. butter and ¼ pint of water, which you season with salt and pepper and bring to the boil, stirring to make sure they are well mixed. Pour in, all at once, 4 tablespoonfuls of flour, and beat well, till the mixture leaves the sides of the saucepan. Remove from the fire and beat in, one by one, 4 eggs. Make sure each is thoroughly amalgamated before adding the next.

'Now stir in 3 oz. gruyère cut into tiny cubes, and arrange the mixture with a spoon round the edge of a sandwich tin (preferably one with a detachable base) so that you have a sort of cake with a hole in the middle. Sprinkle the top with another ounce of cheese similarly cut into cubes. Put into a moderate oven (Reg. 5) and cook for about 35–40 minutes. Turn the oven off and leave the gougère to cook for a further 5–7 minutes to make sure it is absolutely firm, otherwise it will collapse as soon as you take it out. Serve at once.'

STUFFED CABBAGE

When you want to economize on meat and feel that a vegetarian dish isn't quite satisfying enough, try this.

Blanch a cabbage in boiling salted water for 5 minutes, then take it out, drain it and tear off the leaves. Make a stuffing of ½ lb. sausage meat and ½ lb. minced veal; season with thyme, parsley, a little grated nutmeg and garlic, salt and pepper; bind with the yolk of an egg and 2 tablespoonfuls of breadcrumbs and beat all together. Put a layer of the cabbage leaves at the bottom of a casserole, then spread a layer of the stuffing, cover with cabbage leaves and fill up the casserole with alternate layers of stuffing and leaves, finishing with a layer of cabbage. Now stick 2 cloves into the top leaves, and cover with a sauce made from 2 oz. butter, 2 oz. flour, a heaped tablespoonful of tomato purée and ½ pint of stock. Put the lid on the casserole and cook in a slow oven for an hour.

Supper Dishes

VEAL AND HAM CHEESE

Buy the cheapest stewing veal and put 1½ lb. through the mincer, or get the butcher to do it for you. Remove the rind from 4 rashers of unsmoked back bacon, chop into little cubes and mix with the veal. Add ½ cup of breadcrumbs and 2 beaten eggs, and season with thyme (or marjoram), parsley, nutmeg, salt and pepper. Grease an oblong cake tin, press the mixture well in, brush with beaten egg white and sprinkle with breadcrumbs. Dot with bits of butter and bake in a moderate oven (Reg. 5) for an hour. You can eat it hot or cold.

MEXICAN ROLLS

This is quite a good way of using up the remains of a chicken, and again can be eaten hot or cold.

To 2 teacupfuls of mashed potato add a cupful of chopped cooked chicken, a cupful of chopped cooked carrots and 2 tablespoonfuls of stock. Season highly with salt, paprika, grated onion and tabasco. Spread slices of ham very thickly with the mixture, roll, tie with thin string, brush with melted butter or oil, and bake in a moderate oven (Reg. 5) for 25 minutes.

SPAGHETTI BOLOGNESE

When this is made with freshly-minced beef, it bears absolutely no resemblance to the rancid-tasting concoction composed of remains of goodness knows what, flung into stale gravy and served under the name of Spaghetti Bolognese in cheap restaurants.

As a main dish you will need 1 lb. of minced beef. Fry a large chopped onion in 3 tablespoonfuls of oil (olive oil if possible), and when golden add the minced beef and ¼ lb. thinly-sliced mushrooms (use the stalks as well as the caps). Make sure that the beef is properly seized in the oil. It will take about 5 minutes. Now add a glass of red wine and let it boil for a moment or two. Season with salt, pepper and basil, 2 heaped tablespoonfuls of tomato purée, a heaped teaspoonful of sugar and enough water or stock to make a creamy sauce. Cover and cook very gently for 45 minutes.

To cook the spaghetti, allow 2–4 oz. per person. Boil in a large saucepan of salted water for 15–20 minutes. Don't let it get too soft or you will find it turns mushy when drained.

To serve, put the spaghetti into the bottom of a heated dish and pour the sauce over. Serve a bowl of grated parmesan separately.

LAITUES DE LA MÈRE LANDURETTE

I think too few people are aware of the delicate flavour of lettuces when cooked. Try this when you have some remains of chicken or veal.

Allow 1 lettuce to each ½ lb. of minced meat. Blanch the lettuce in salted water for a minute and carefully tear off the leaves. In a basin mix the minced meat with 5 tablespoonfuls of uncooked rice and an egg. Season with salt and pepper. Put spoonfuls of this mixture on to each lettuce leaf, and roll into little packets. Place the rolls in a dish and pour over a carton of cream and bake in a moderate oven (Reg. 5) for 45 minutes. Take a look half-way through and if the rolls are beginning to look dry, add 2 or 3 spoonfuls of stock.

PILAF À LA REINE

Cook 8 tablespoonfuls of rice in salted water. Drain and put in a dish, then cover and leave in a slow oven (Reg. 1) for 25 minutes. In the meantime make a Béchamel with 1 oz. butter, a level tablespoonful of flour and ½ pint of chicken stock. Add the chopped remains of a chicken, ½ lb. thinly-sliced mushrooms and a pinch of saffron or curry powder. Leave to cook gently for 20 minutes. Add a small carton of cream, mix with the rice, check the seasoning and serve well sprinkled with chopped parsley.

PORK WITH JAMBALAYA RICE

Cut 4 oz. fat bacon into dice and heat in a frying-pan. When the fat starts to run, add 2 chopped onions. When golden, remove these and the bacon and fry all over a piece of pork weighing about 1 lb. When the pork is well browned, return the pieces of bacon and onion and add 4 oz. chopped ham. Moisten with 2 pints of stock. Boil for 15 minutes. Lower the heat and add 8 tablespoonfuls of well-washed rice, a bouquet of herbs and salt and cayenne pepper. Cook for a further 10 minutes.

GÂTEAU DE VOLAILLE À LA CRÈME

This is not only a delicious way of cooking a rather aged boiling fowl, but it is a most economical dish to serve at a buffet party.

Boil a large bird, seasoning well with salt and pepper and a bouquet of herbs. When cooked, leave to cool in the stock. Make a very thick Béchamel with 3 oz. butter, 3 tablespoonfuls of flour and a pint of the chicken stock, strained. Add a packet of aspic jelly (Maggi does an excellent one au madère), and a small carton of cream and cook for a few more minutes. Cut the chicken into pieces that can be easily speared on a fork and stir into the sauce. If you like you can add a handful of cooked young peas and some cooked new carrots, cut into little rounds. Rinse a soufflé dish in cold water, pour in the mixture and leave in the fridge for at least 3 hours. To serve, turn out on to a flat dish. The only accompaniment you need is a well-seasoned green salad.

Hors-d'oeuvre and Salads

Rillettes de porc • Terrine de campagne • Fromage de porc en salade • Riz à l'orientale • Oignons à la monégasque • Salade de lentilles aux chipolatas • Salade niçoise • Céleri-rave rémoulade • Salade de céleri • Salade de tomates • Salade Rachel • Salade de champignons • Salade de champignons aux bananes • Champignons à la Grecque • Cole Slaw • Salade d'endives et de betteraves • Oeufs durs à la mayonnaise • Pain d'aubergines • Avocado and orange

Hors-d'oeuvre and Salads

❖❖❖❖❖❖❖❖❖❖❖❖❖❖❖❖❖❖❖❖❖❖❖❖❖❖❖❖❖❖❖❖❖❖❖❖❖❖❖

In most French homes the basic hors-d'oeuvre consists of a
tomato salad, a dish of little pink radishes, and some slices of
either saucisson, or one of the many pâtés or country terrines,
either cut in slices or served direct from the earthenware
terrine they have been cooked in.

Although most delicatessen shops stock either pâtés in tins
or good commercially-made untinned ones, nothing really
tastes like home-made *charcuterie*. I am therefore including a
few recipes which are neither long nor trying to make. Most
of them will keep well in the fridge and they are a very good
standby to offer when you are faced with providing a meal
for the unexpected guest.

RILLETTES DE PORC

This is one of the classic hors-d'oeuvre and is found all over
France. The rillettes are quite easy to make, and although the
standard recipes use only pork, I find a mixture of pork and
duck or rabbit, for instance, far less insipid.

Buy 2 lb. belly pork and 1 lb. bacon (the amount of fat and
lean should be about equal). Get your butcher to remove any
bones. Chop the meat into pieces, together with any other
meat you are going to use, and put them in an earthenware
casserole with salt, pepper, bay leaf, thyme, a clove of garlic
and a pinch each of nutmeg, cinnamon and cloves. Add

enough water to half-cover the meat. Put the lid on the casserole, and cook as slowly as possible (either on top of the stove or in the oven (Reg. 1) for 4 hours, when the water should be more or less evaporated and the meat reduced almost to a purée, and swimming in fat. Strain off the fat and put the meat into a basin. Beat all together, with a fork. It should be well amalgamated, but not a purée. You can either store the rillettes in small soufflé dishes or pack them into earthenware basins. In any case, cover them with the strained fat, which you remove before serving.

TERRINE DE CAMPAGNE

Mince very finely 1 lb. belly pork and 1 lb. veal. Buy a truffle (it will keep for months if you put it in a jar with a little brandy), and cut a few slivers which you then chop and mix with your minced meat. Chop into little dice 6 oz. unsmoked bacon and add to the mixture. Season with very little salt, pepper, nutmeg and marjoram, a grated clove of garlic and 2 tablespoonfuls of brandy. You can either pack this mixture as it is into your terrine or put it with alternate layers of thin slices of chicken, duck or rabbit. Lay a bay leaf on top and cover with thin strips of streaky bacon crisscrossed. If your terrine has no lid, seal with foil. Place a tin with enough water to come half-way up the sides of the terrine and cook in a very slow oven (Reg. 3) for about 1½ hours. Leave to go cold. You can either serve it as it is, or take it out of the dish.

FROMAGE DE PORC EN SALADE

This is a rather refined version of brawn, and is sold by *charcutiers* in slices marinated in oil and coarsely chopped parsley and onion.

Buy 2 lb. salt pork, or you can use a pig's cheek and 1 lb. of the pork. Soak the meat for an hour and then put it into a saucepan with a large onion, 2 carrots, a bouquet of plenty of parsley stalks, thyme and bay leaf and half a dozen peppercorns. Cover with cold water and add a tablespoonful of vinegar. Put the lid on the saucepan and cook very gently for 1½–2 hours. The meat should then be quite soft. Remove it, pour over it a tablespoonful of oil and put it into a dish of a size and shape which will make it easy to cut into slices when turned out. Leave overnight, with a weight on top to press it into shape.

The next day cut it into thin slices and cover with a vinaigrette sauce made with a small onion finely chopped, ½ teaspoonful of French mustard, and oil and vinegar in the proportion of 1 part of vinegar to 5 parts of oil. Sprinkle with plenty of chopped parsley.

RIZ À L'ORIENTALE

Dissolve ½ teaspoonful of saffron in 6 tablespoonfuls of white wine and a pint of chicken bouillon. Add a green pimento with the seeds removed, finely chopped, 12 tablespoonfuls of rice, ½ teaspoonful of caraway seeds and a small chopped onion. Season with salt and pepper. Turn all into a saucepan and cook gently till all the liquid is absorbed. While still warm, mix with a dressing of a dessertspoonful of vinegar and 3 tablespoonfuls of oil. Chill and serve sprinkled with chopped parsley.

OIGNONS À LA MONÉGASQUE

The preparation of this is a bit fiddling, but the result will amply repay the trouble you take.

Use the small round onions used for pickling. First chop a carrot into small dice and cook in 2 tablespoonfuls of oil till soft. Then add 1 lb. peeled onions, 2 chopped tomatoes, a bouquet of parsley, thyme and bay leaf, a heaped tablespoonful of currants, a teaspoonful of vinegar and ½ pint of water. Season and simmer till the onions are soft and the sauce has thickened. Chill before serving.

SALADE DE LENTILLES AUX CHIPOLATAS

Buy the brown lentils which are obtainable at most continental stores. Soak 6 oz. in cold water for 12 hours.

Chop an onion and sweat it in 2 tablespoonfuls of oil. Add a clove of garlic, a bay leaf, salt and 2 pints of water. Put the strained lentils into this stock, cover, and cook gently for 1½–2 hours. Drain the lentils well, and while they are still warm make the following dressing. Put a teaspoonful of French mustard in the bottom of a basin, then stir into it salt and freshly-ground black pepper, a tablespoonful of vinegar, a tablespoonful of lemon juice and 4 tablespoonfuls of oil. When thickened and well amalgamated, mix with the lentils. Serve with chipolata sausages grilled and left to get cold.

SALADE NIÇOISE

This is one of the great classic hors-d'oeuvre and, though its origin is Mediterranean, it is eaten all over France, the variations in the vegetables depending on the season and the region. Here is a fairly representative version, which makes quite a substantial first course to any meal.

Cook ½ lb. haricots verts (the smallest you can get) and let them get cold. Mix them with a vinaigrette made with a tablespoonful of vinegar and 5 tablespoonfuls of olive oil. Put the beans in the centre of your salad bowl, and arrange about 3 oz. olives round them. Arrange on top a dozen fillets of anchovy and you can add, too, a small tin of tunny fish well drained and chopped into cubes. Sprinkle with a teaspoonful of capers, and any vinaigrette remaining. Decorate with slices of hard-boiled egg.

CÉLERI-RAVE RÉMOULADE

Peel the celeriac root, and cut it into fine matchstick strips. Throw into boiling salted water and blanch for 5 minutes. Drain and wipe well in an old tea towel. While still warm, mix with a sauce rémoulade (see page 146).

SALADE DE CÉLERI

Crisp a head of celery in ice water and chop finely. Peel a couple of dessert apples (Worcesters or Cox's Orange Pippins) and mix all together with a rather mustardy mayonnaise. Sprinkle with chopped parsley before serving.

SALADE DE TOMATES

Plunge the tomatoes for half a minute in boiling water to loosen the skins. Remove skins and slice thinly into rounds. If you can lay your hands on some chives, nothing could be nicer, but if not use a few rings of onion and toss in a well salted vinaigrette. Sprinkle with chopped parsley.

SALADE RACHEL

In the winter, when green salads are expensive, try this for a change.

Prepare a vinaigrette. Chop 3 or 4 sticks of celery and marinate in the vinaigrette for an hour. Then add a chopped crisp dessert apple, a chopped Belgian endive and about a dozen walnuts, shelled, skinned and roughly chopped. Mix all well and turn into a salad bowl. Decorate with thin rounds of beetroot sprinkled with chopped parsley.

SALADE DE CHAMPIGNONS

Wash the mushrooms, cut off the ends of the stalks and slice thinly. Drain well and mix with a dressing of 2 tablespoonfuls of oil, the juice of half a lemon and salt and pepper. Sprinkle with plenty of chopped parsley.

SALADE DE CHAMPIGNONS AUX BANANES

Prepare the mushrooms as in the previous recipe. For ½ lb. mushrooms you will need 2 bananas. Choose ones which are not too ripe. Skin them and slice in thin rounds. Mix with the mushrooms, and toss in a sauce made with 2 tablespoons of cream, the juice of a lemon, salt and freshly-ground pepper.

CHAMPIGNONS À LA GRECQUE

Many vegetables take kindly to this method of preparation, among them artichokes, the white part of leeks, celery and fennel roots.

For ½ lb. mushrooms, prepare a sauce as follows. Put in a saucepan a small wineglassful of olive oil, the same quantity of water, and the same of dry white wine, with a couple of small tomatoes, skinned and roughly chopped, 10 coriander seeds, a small bunch of thyme and a bay leaf, salt and pepper. Boil fast for 2 or 3 minutes. Reduce the heat, squeeze in the juice of half a lemon and add the mushrooms. Cook gently uncovered, till the mushrooms have softened (but they must not be soft!). Turn into a dish and chill.

COLE SLAW

Here is another salad for the winter months.

Shred half a head of white cabbage, removing the hard stalky parts, and crisp in cold water for half an hour. Drain well, then marinate for an hour in a tablespoonful of sugar, 4 tablespoonfuls of vinegar and a dusting of paprika. Make a very stiff mayonnaise and add 2 tablespoonfuls of single cream and ¼ teaspoonful of caraway seeds. Remove the cabbage from the marinade, drain thoroughly and fold gently into the mayonnaise. The longer in advance it is prepared, the better it will be.

SALADE D'ENDIVES ET DE BETTERAVES

Slice the endives and amalgamate with a rather salty vinaigrette made with a teaspoonful of vinegar and 3 tablespoonfuls of oil. Just before serving, add some beetroot cut into match-sized strips.

OEUFS DURS À LA MAYONNAISE

Allow 1 egg per person. Boil them for 10 minutes, plunge in cold water and remove the shells. Slice in half lengthwise. Spread a layer of mayonnaise on a shallow dish and arrange the eggs yolk-side down, strew over a few capers and a liberal sprinkling of chopped parsley.

PAIN D'AUBERGINES

Allow 1 aubergine per person. For four, slice aubergines lengthwise, score, lightly sprinkle with salt and bake in the oven (Reg. 4) till the flesh is soft, about 15–20 minutes. Scoop out the flesh. Put 2 tablespoonfuls of oil in a frying-pan, and fry a finely-chopped onion and a minced clove of garlic. Add 4 peeled and chopped tomatoes and the aubergine flesh. Season with salt, pepper and marjoram. Cook slowly, stirring frequently, till the aubergine flesh has become almost a purée and completely amalgamated with the other ingredients. Chill and serve with a bowl of black olives.

AVOCADO AND ORANGE

Quite a number of people find avocado pear disagreeably rich at the beginning of a meal. The combination of its rather fatty flesh with the acidity of orange not only makes a pleasant change from the usual preparation, but will certainly ensure that there are no digestive ill-effects.

Cut the pears in half lengthways in the usual way, allowing half a pear per person. Skin an equal number of oranges and cut similarly. Lay the pears flat side down on the plates on which you are going to serve them, and slice them across in four pieces. Cut the oranges similarly. Slip a slice of orange in between each piece of avocado and press gently together so that you have a reconstituted and rather elongated striped pear.

Serve with a lemon dressing made with a dessertspoon of lemon juice to 3 tablespoonfuls of oil. No salt. Pour over the pears at the last moment.

Vegetables

Pommes de terre au basilic • Pommes de terre Macaire • Pommes de terre à la Lyonnaise • Gratin Savoyard • Aubergines farcies Marcelle • Aubergines aux tomates • Aubergines frites • Carottes à la Vichy • Timbale de carottes • Braised celery • Red cabbage • Brussels Sprouts with chestnuts • Bubble and Squeak • Cauliflower à la Polonaise • Cauliflower au gratin • Broad beans • Courgettes sautées aux fines herbes • Courgettes à la crème • Courgettes aux tomates • Endives • Épinards à la crème • Épinards aux oeufs durs • Haricots blancs à la bretonne • Braised lettuce • Braised onions • Poireaux à l'étuvée • Petits pois à la française • Pumpkin purée • Stuffed tomatoes

Vegetables

✤·❊·✤

In France, vegetables are as often served as a separate course
as they are as an accompaniment to another dish. I have
therefore included a number of 'plats de légumes cuisinés'—
an expression used to describe a composition of more than
one ingredient. When you are serving one very expensive
fish or meat course, a cheap vegetable course makes a perfect
beginning to a meal.

POMMES DE TERRE AU BASILIC

Peel some potatoes, preferably the long Dutch waxy kind,
and slice in rounds about ¼ in. thick. For a pound of potatoes
melt 2 oz. butter in ½ tumbler of water, with salt, pepper
and a good sprinkling of dried basil. Put in the potatoes so
that they cover the bottom of the pan, and cook them slowly,
shaking the pan from time to time to make sure they are not
sticking. Turn them out, with what remains of the liquid. It
will have been considerably reduced.

POMMES DE TERRE MACAIRE

Choose large floury potatoes. Wash them and bake them in
their skins in the oven (Reg. 6) for about 45 minutes. When
cooked, remove the skins and mash the potatoes with a fork,
incorporating 2 oz. butter for each pound of purée. Season

with salt, pepper and grated nutmeg. Heat a nut of butter in a
frying-pan. Spread the purée over the pan about an inch
thick. When the bottom side is a good golden colour, lift
with a slice, while you slip into the pan another nut of butter.
Let it melt completely before you brown the other side of
your potato galette. Serve at once.

POMMES DE TERRE À LA LYONNAISE

Boil some Dutch potatoes in their jackets and leave to grow
cold before you skin them. Cut into rounds ¼ in. thick. Melt
1½ oz. butter in a frying-pan and cook the potatoes gently. In
another pan do the same with 2 onions, similarly sliced and
seasoned with salt and pepper. When the onions begin to
colour, add them to the potatoes and continue cooking for
another 10 minutes. Serve with plenty of chopped parsley.

GRATIN SAVOYARD

Peel some potatoes, wash them well and cut them into dice.
Butter a flame-proof dish, put in half the potatoes and
sprinkle thickly with grated cheese (preferably Gruyère), adding salt, pepper and grated nutmeg. Repeat the process till
the dish is full, ending with a layer of cheese. Moisten with
stock, dot with butter and cook on the top of the stove for 10
minutes. Then put into a moderate oven (Reg. 6) for about
half an hour when the top should be golden brown and the
stock evaporated.

AUBERGINES FARCIES MARCELLE

Allow 1 aubergine per person. Cut each in half lengthwise,
score, sprinkle with salt and put in the oven (Reg. 4) till the
flesh is soft. This will take about 15 minutes.

Meanwhile prepare the stuffing. For 4 aubergines skin and chop 3 medium tomatoes and put them into a saucepan. Clean and chop $\frac{1}{4}$ lb. mushrooms and add them to the tomatoes. Now stir in a tablespoonful of cream, an ounce of butter and a tablespoonful of tomato purée. Season with salt, pepper, grated nutmeg and chopped parsley and thyme. Cook slowly, and add a tablespoonful of chopped pine kernels if you can get them. If not, use peanuts. Continue cooking until the mixture has thickened and leaves the side of the pan. Remove from the fire and stir in a tablespoonful of breadcrumbs and another tablespoonful of cream.

Scrape out the flesh from the aubergines, chop it up and stir it into the pan with the stuffing. Simmer another 5 minutes, then fill the skins with the mixture. Dot with butter and brown under the grill.

AUBERGINES AUX TOMATES

Allow 1 aubergine per person. First prepare a tomato purée. For 4 aubergines, cut $1\frac{1}{2}$ lb. tomatoes in quarters, cook them without water or any other liquid for 10 minutes and put them through a sieve. Fry in oil the aubergines, cut into thick rounds. In a fireproof dish arrange a layer of the tomato purée, then a layer of the aubergines, seasoning each layer with parsley, salt and finely-minced garlic, till the dish is full. Dot with pieces of butter and cook in the oven (Reg. 5) for 45 minutes.

AUBERGINES FRITES

Skin the aubergines and slice in rounds $\frac{1}{4}$ in. thick. Sprinkle with salt and leave in a colander to drain for half an hour. When ready to cook, make sure the slices are dry. Roll in seasoned flour and fry in very hot oil till golden. Serve strewn with minced parsley.

CAROTTES À LA VICHY

For 4 people scrape 1½ lb. carrots, wash them well and slice them in very thin rounds. Put them into a saucepan and add cold water so that it almost covers the carrots, 3½ oz. butter, salt and 4 lumps of sugar. Cover, and boil fast till the water has boiled away and you can hear the carrots beginning to sizzle in the fat. They will now be cooked. Sprinkle with chopped parsley and serve at once.

TIMBALE DE CAROTTES

Grate enough carrot to fill 2 teacups. Add 4 well-beaten eggs, 4 tablespoonfuls of melted butter, a little grated onion, salt, pepper, 2 tablespoonfuls of thick cream and a tablespoonful of flour. Mix well and turn into a well-greased soufflé dish. Cover with foil, set in a baking tin half filled with water and bake in the oven (Reg. 5) till firm (about 35 minutes).

BRAISED CELERY

Personally I am not very fond of cooked celery, but with certain game no other vegetable seems to go as well. This makes a good accompaniment to pheasant.

Blanch 3 heads of celery in boiling salted water for 10 minutes. Take out and drain thoroughly. Brown lightly in butter 2 sliced onions and 2 sliced carrots. Add the celery and season with salt and pepper. Pour on ½ pint of stock and simmer gently for an hour. If you have any juice from a joint (sometimes found at the bottom of a basin of dripping), now is the time to add it. Cook for a further 10 minutes and serve.

RED CABBAGE

Melt an ounce of dripping in a saucepan. When hot, add 1 lb. red cabbage, shredded, a large sliced onion, a large cooking apple, peeled, cored and chopped, 2 tablespoonfuls of stock, 2 tablespoonfuls of vinegar, a tablespoonful of demerara sugar, and salt and pepper. Stir, so that all the ingredients are coated with the fat and stock, then cover and simmer for 30–45 minutes. Stir occasionally. The liquid should have almost entirely evaporated by the end of the cooking.

BRUSSELS SPROUTS WITH CHESTNUTS

Prepare the chestnuts as indicated on page 54. Boil the brussels sprouts (they should take about 20 minutes, no longer or they will lose their colour), mix with the chestnuts and add an ounce of melted butter before serving.

Very good with roast turkey or pheasant.

BUBBLE AND SQUEAK

When we were children, this was almost our favourite vegetable.

Boil a cabbage, drain it well and chop it very small. At the same time boil half the weight of the cabbage in potatoes, drain and mash well with a fork. In a frying-pan brown a thinly sliced onion in plenty of beef dripping, then add the potatoes and cabbage, with seasoning, and mix well. When the underside of the cake is well browned, turn it out.

CAULIFLOWER À LA POLONAISE

This accompaniment makes a pleasant change from the taste-less white sauce so often served with cauliflower.

Soak the cauliflower for 10 minutes in water to which you have added a spoonful of vinegar. Cauliflower is rather tricky to cook, for if you are not careful you will find you have a collection of stalks and disintegrated flowerets. Cook the cauliflower head upwards in a covered pan in boiling salted water. At the end of 10 minutes the flowerets should be almost soft. Turn off the heat and leave it to finish cooking in its own steam. Turn it carefully into a colander and drain. Keep it warm. In a pan put a good piece of butter and let it become golden. At this point throw in a handful of breadcrumbs and cook till crisp and brown. Pour the crumbs and butter over the cauliflower and sprinkle with some chopped ham, hard-boiled egg and plenty of parsley.

CAULIFLOWER AU GRATIN

The secret of making this sauce something more than an ordinary cheese-flavoured Béchamel is to use the water you have cooked the cauliflower in, with the addition of 2 or 3 spoonfuls of cream and a good grating of nutmeg.

Cook the cauliflower as in the previous recipe, but save the stock. Make the sauce with an ounce of butter, a tablespoonful of flour and ¾ pint of the cauliflower stock. When well amalgamated, stir in 3 good tablespoonfuls of grated cheese and the cream. Pour it over the cauliflower, strew over some breadcrumbs and more grated cheese and brown in the oven for 10 minutes.

BROAD BEANS

In the part of France where I live, young broad beans are eaten raw, as an hors-d'oeuvre; or cooked in their pods; or when they are old, they are puréed and used for soup. Need-

less to say, there are many other ways of cooking this delicious vegetable, though when they are young nothing is
nicer than the freshly-boiled beans tossed in butter and well
sprinkled with parsley.

When they are getting large and old, and if you have the
time, remove the skins, which by now are tough and inclined
to be bitter, and cook beans only as above; or serve them in a
purée, made by sieving the beans (shelled and boiled of
course), and beating up with butter and a little stock.

One of the classic ways of serving broad beans is to mix
them with bacon cut into cubes, the fat from the bacon, a
spoonful or two of cream, and some chopped parsley.

COURGETTES SAUTÉES AUX FINES HERBES

If the courgettes are small, use them without peeling, but if
more than 5 inches long, peel thinly, salt, and leave to drain
for an hour. Let them sauté gently in butter for 10 minutes,
then season with salt and pepper, and chopped parsley, tarragon and chervil.

COURGETTES À LA CRÈME

Cook the courgettes as above, and before serving add 2 or 3
tablespoonfuls of cream, a little finely-grated raw carrot and
some chopped chives. Shake the pan before serving.

COURGETTES AUX TOMATES

Salt and drain the courgettes as above and cook gently in
butter for 10 minutes. Now add 3 or 4 small tomatoes,
skinned and sliced into rounds. Simmer for another 10
minutes and serve immediately.

ENDIVES

(In England this vegetable is often called chicory.)

You can either boil the endives and finish cooking them in butter, or (and I prefer this method) you can put 1 lb. into a casserole, pour on 2 oz. melted butter and add salt, pepper and the juice of half a lemon. Cover, and cook in the oven (Reg. 3) for at least an hour, when the outside leaves should be golden and all the liquid evaporated.

ÉPINARDS À LA CRÈME

Spinach reduces enormously in cooking so you must allow at least ½ lb. per person. Remove the stalks and wash the leaves well in several waters to remove every trace of grit or sand. Put them without any other water into a saucepan and add salt. As the water from the leaves starts to boil, press the spinach well, so that all the leaves are well covered, and boil for 10 minutes. Drain well and press out the water with your hands. For 2 lb. spinach, melt 2 oz. butter and add the spinach and a carton of cream. Check the seasoning, and stir in a tiny grating of nutmeg and a pinch of sugar. Turn the spinach well over in the creamy sauce and serve at once.

ÉPINARDS AUX OEUFS DURS

This makes a most excellent first course, or, if you make enough, a delicious supper dish.

Prepare the spinach as in the previous recipe, and at the same time hard-boil some eggs. To serve, put the spinach in a mound in the centre of the dish, quarter the eggs and arrange them all round, and decorate with little piles of triangular pieces of bread fried very crisp in oil.

HARICOTS BLANCS À LA BRETONNE

These are the traditional accompaniment to roast lamb, but they are most warm and comforting to eat in the winter. Serve them with frankfurters, or any other kind of sausage.

Make sure when you buy the beans that they are new season's. Take a bean and put it between your teeth. If fresh you will be able to bite it quite easily, but if old it will be as hard as a stone and no amount of cooking will soften it.

Put $\frac{1}{2}$ lb. haricots into cold water and bring to the boil. Throw the water away and put the beans back into fresh water so that they are well covered. Add a bouquet of herbs, an onion stuck with a clove, and a carrot. Cover and cook gently for at least 2 hours. You can do this the day before you want to use the beans. When cooked, drain them and keep the liquid. Fry a chopped onion in butter, or better still some dripping, and add 2 or 3 peeled and chopped tomatoes. Add a little of the bean liquid to make a thinnish sauce. Check the seasoning, put the beans back into the sauce, mix well and serve.

BRAISED LETTUCE

Use small outdoor lettuces for this and serve them, as a change from other vegetables, with roast veal. Cut the lettuces in half and let them sauté in butter. Add a little stock, or better still some juice from the roast, and cook with the lid on until the lettuces are soft and the liquid in the pan is well reduced, about 10–15 minutes. Squeeze a little lemon juice over and sprinkle with chopped parsley.

BRAISED ONIONS

Choose onions as much the same size as possible and brown them well in butter. Remove them on to a plate and when the butter is a good brown, stir in a dessertspoonful of flour until amalgamated and then pour in enough stock and a glass of white wine to make a thin sauce. Return the onions to the pan, see that they are well coated, cover and cook in the oven (Reg. 3) for about an hour, when the sauce should be thickened and reduced.

POIREAUX À L'ÉTUVÉE

Wash some leeks, discard the pithy outside leaves and chop into rounds about an inch long. Drain well, and sweat them in butter. Season with salt and pepper, cover, and cook for 10 minutes. Add 2 or 3 tomatoes, skinned and sliced into rounds, and the juice of half a lemon, and cook for a further 10 minutes. Arrange the leeks on a dish and if the sauce is too thin, reduce by boiling fiercely for a minute or two.

PETITS POIS À LA FRANÇAISE

Put the raw peas into a saucepan with a good lump of butter. Allow the butter to melt and incorporate it well with the peas, then add the bulbs of some spring onions and a small handful of chopped lettuce. Season with salt, pepper and a teaspoonful of sugar. Pour in enough water to reach just to the top of the peas, cover, and cook for about 30 minutes, when most of the liquid should have evaporated.

PUMPKIN PURÉE

As this is another very watery vegetable, you will need 2 lb. for 4 people. Peel and cut into convenient pieces, and cook in salted water till soft. Drain, and pass the flesh through a sieve then return it to the saucepan and mix with 2 oz. butter.

Check seasoning and grate a little nutmeg into the purée. Stir in 2 well beaten eggs, dot over with little pieces of butter and put in a hot oven to brown, about 10–12 minutes. Serve quickly, as it will have risen rather like a soufflé.

STUFFED TOMATOES

Cut the tops off large tomatoes (allow 2 per person), and scoop out the flesh with a spoon. Turn the tomatoes upside down on a plate and allow them to drain for half an hour. You can then put them as they are into the fridge until you are ready to fill them.

For 8 tomatoes you will need ½ lb. sausage meat, mixed with ½ lb. minced cooked remains of a joint. Stir in a tablespoonful of chopped parsley, and salt and pepper. If the mixture seems too dry, moisten with a little meat stock. Fill the emptied tomatoes. Stand them in a shallow fireproof dish, strew some crisp breadcrumbs over the stuffing in each tomato and pour on a teaspoonful of oil. Bake in the oven (Reg. 6) for half an hour.

Use the tomato flesh for either a tomato sauce, a soup or a tarte aux tomates.

Sweets

Pastry
Short crust ◆ *Pâte brisée* ◆ *Pâte à choux*

Sweets with No Eggs
Fried-apple tart ◆ *Apple Charlotte* ◆ *Spiced baked apples* ◆ *Apple crumble* ◆ *Poires au vin* ◆ *Gooseberry fool* ◆ *Gooseberry cheese* ◆ *Émincés de poires* ◆ *Vanilla cream* ◆ *Turinois*

Sweets with Whole Eggs
Profiterolles au chocolat ◆ *Nègre en chemise* ◆ *Mousse au chocolat* ◆ *Cold orange soufflé* ◆ *Cold nut soufflé* ◆ *Gâteau de fromage blanc* ◆ *Lemon fluff* ◆ *Oeufs à la neige* ◆ *Crèmes frites* ◆ *Pain perdu* ◆ *Potato pudding* ◆ *Walmer pudding*

Sweets with Egg Yolks
Crème anglaise ◆ *Crème pâtissière* ◆ *Café parfait* ◆ *Petits pots de crème à la vanille* ◆ *Gâteau viennois*

Sweets with Egg Whites
Visitandines ◆ *Financiers* ◆ *Mousse au chocolat* ◆ *Flaméri de semoule* ◆ *Mousse aux fraises*

Sweets

❖❖❖❖❖❖❖❖❖❖❖❖❖❖❖❖❖❖❖❖❖❖❖❖❖❖❖❖❖❖❖❖❖❖❖

PASTRY

I have intentionally given no recipes for flaky pastry. For those of you who want to attempt it, most standard cookery books provide quantities and method. But to make really satisfactory flaky pastry it is essential to have a cool kitchen and plenty of time. The purpose of this book is to give recipes easy and reasonably quick to prepare. There are a number of reliable brands of prepared flaky pastry, which can be bought in most supermarkets, good grocers and delicatessen, and which only need rolling out.

However, I do want to give two foolproof pastry recipes; one for short crust, the pastry used for quiches, and the other a pâte brisée for fruit tarts. And I want to give, too, a recipe for pâte à choux, essential for éclairs, cheese buns and profiterolles.

SHORT CRUST

8 heaped tablespoonfuls flour	1 saltspoonful salt
¼ lb. margarine (this makes much lighter pastry than butter)	1 level tablespoonful sugar (omitted in the case of savoury tarts)
	¾ tumblerful water

Sieve the flour into a basin, make a well in the middle, break up the fat and place it in the well, together with the other

113

ingredients. Knead the mixture with your hands, but not too hard, or it will become elastic and tough when cooked. When smooth and well mixed, roll it into a ball, wrap in a cloth or foil paper and leave in the fridge at least an hour before using. It can be made the day before.

PÂTE BRISÉE

8 heaped tablespoonfuls flour   ¼ lb. margarine
A pinch of salt   1 tablespoonful oil
Water

Sieve the flour into a basin. Make a hole in the middle and put in the oil, the salt and the fat, cut into little pieces. Work these ingredients lightly with the tips of the fingers until the mixture looks like breadcrumbs. Moisten with a little water, and mix to a paste with a knife. Knead with the palm of your hand. The whole operation should be done as quickly as possible and the pastry can be left up to 3 days in the fridge if you roll it into a ball and keep it covered. To use, roll out as required on a floured surface.

PÂTE À CHOUX

Bring to the boil a breakfast cup of water, 3 oz. butter and a pinch of salt. Pour in, all at once, 4 heaped tablespoonfuls of flour. Beat well till the mixture leaves the sides of the pan. Remove from the heat, cool for a minute and then add, one by one, 4 eggs, making sure to beat each one well in before adding the next. The result should be a softish but pliable paste. If the eggs are big ones, you will probably find you will not need the fourth, so do not break it before the other 3 are well mixed in.

This pastry should be used straight away.

SWEETS WITH NO EGGS

FRIED-APPLE TART

My sons, who are not greatly addicted to cooked apples, having had a surfeit of various forms of stodgy apple puddings at school, nevertheless adore this sweet, which is particularly delicious when the first Worcesters, and, a little later, the first Cox's appear in the shops.

Peel and core about 1½ lb. apples and slice evenly and thinly. Cook very gently in 2 oz. butter and 2 tablespoonfuls caster sugar in a frying-pan. Line a sandwich tin (preferably one with a removable base) with short crust pastry or pâte brisée. (See the recipes in the previous section.) Arrange the apples in overlapping rounds. Save the juice in the frying-pan. Bake for 30–35 minutes in a hot oven (Reg. 6) and pour the juice over just before serving.

When I have no time to make pastry, I fry fingers of bread in very hot oil, arrange the apples similarly and serve with cream.

APPLE CHARLOTTE

For some reason, this delicious pudding seems to have gone out of fashion, and although it isn't exactly the thing to serve at a particularly sophisticated dinner party, it makes a most satisfactory finale to an informal cold supper.

Cut some slices of bread into strips the depth of a soufflé dish (which is the ideal shape for this sweet), and about 1½ in. wide. Cut also a number of triangular or narrow kite-shaped slices to cover the bottom of the mould, which should be well greased with butter. Dip the pieces of bread in melted butter, and place the triangular pieces in the form of a circle, with the points meeting in the centre. Then fix the fingers similarly against the sides of the mould. Fill the mould with a fairly stiff apple purée made from 1½ lb. apples cooked, unpeeled and uncored, in a little water, then passed through the smallest mesh of the food mill and flavoured with sugar, lemon juice, a little grated lemon peel and a pinch of ground cinnamon. Trim off any strips of bread that project over the top of the mould, and lay 3 or 4 strips across the top of the apple. Bake in a hot oven (Reg. 6) for about 40 minutes, when the bread should be golden and crisp. Serve at once, with cream.

SPICED BAKED APPLES

Cream together (for 4 large apples) 2 oz. butter and 2 oz. brown sugar, beat in ½ teaspoonful of ground cinnamon and 1 teaspoonful of grated lemon peel. Core the apples and fill with the butter cream. Top with a clove. Place in a shallow oven dish and pour on the top of each apple a teaspoonful of golden syrup and a tablespoonful of lemon juice. Bake in a moderate oven (Reg. 5) for 40 minutes.

APPLE CRUMBLE

This is an ideal winter sweet, which does not suffer from being warmed up.

Cut into quarters, without peeling, 1½ lb. cooking apples and put into a saucepan with a tumblerful of water, 2 tablespoonfuls of brown sugar and a tablespoonful of golden syrup. Cook with the lid on until the apples are soft, then put them through the medium mesh of the food mill. While the apples are cooking, put 6 tablespoonfuls of flour in a basin, and rub into it 3 oz. butter, till it resembles breadcrumbs. Pour the apple purée into a pie dish or other conveniently shaped oven dish, and scatter the 'breadcrumbs' thickly over it. Bake in a hot oven (Reg. 6) till crisp and brown (about 30 minutes).

POIRES AU VIN

Peel the pears, leaving the stalks on. For 1 lb. pears, allow a tumblerful of red wine and 4 oz. caster sugar. Stand the pears up in a deep earthenware dish. Pour over them the wine and sugar, and add enough water to reach half-way up the pears. Put them, uncovered, into the slowest possible oven and bake until soft. Look at them from time to time and turn them so that they are impregnated all over with the wine. When done they should be almost mahogany coloured. If dessert pears are used they will take 1–1½ hours. Cooking pears may take anything up to 4 or 5 hours. You can leave them in the oven perfectly safely all day, but they should be served very cold, with the syrup poured over them.

GOOSEBERRY FOOL

When gooseberries are small, green and very acid you can make a quick and utterly delectable sweet by putting a pound of them into a saucepan, with a very little water, and cooking without any sugar until soft. Pass through the finest mesh of the food mill, allow to cool off and fold the purée into a block of ice-cream.

GOOSEBERRY CHEESE

When ice-cream is not available, try this version.

Cook the fruit with 4 tablespoonfuls of sugar, but without

water, and pass through the food mill as above. Mix with a cream cheese made as follows. Buy ½ lb. cream cheese (petits-suisses are quite good to use if you cannot find a suitable one by the pound). Beat it up with a tablespoonful of sugar until smooth. Spread a piece of muslin (a fine handkerchief will do) over the inside of a fairly large strainer and lay the cheese in it. Place the strainer over a basin and allow to drip for an hour or so in a cool place, or in the fridge. When ready to incorporate with the gooseberries, beat the two together until completely amalgamated and add a carton of thick cream.

The cheese is also delicious served as an accompaniment to raspberries and redcurrants, or stewed blackcurrants.

ÉMINCÉS DE POIRES

For this you will need fairly ripe pears. Peel 6 pears, remove the cores, and cut into quarters. Heat 3 oz. butter in a frying-pan and put the fruit in to sauter, taking care not to let it burn. Lay each quarter pear on a finger of bread fried in butter until golden. Serve very hot, sprinkled with sugar.

VANILLA CREAM

When stocks are low and the unexpected guest turns up, this is easily made, and will maintain your reputation for conjuring an epicurean meal out of almost nothing.

For 4 people whip ¼ pint of cream and mix it gradually with ¾ pint of milk. Add a tablespoonful of caster sugar and a teaspoonful of vanilla essence. Dissolve ½ oz. (1 tablespoonful) gelatine in ½ gill of warm water and strain carefully into the cream. Pour into a glass dish and chill in the fridge for an hour.

TURINOIS

This is a sweet to serve after a light main course.

Buy 1½ lb. chestnuts and make an incision with a sharp knife in each one. Scald them. You should then be able to remove the shells. Throw them into boiling water and cook until they are soft enough to skin. Drain well and put through a sieve. While the purée is still hot, beat into it ¼ lb. butter, ¼ lb. grated bitter chocolate and 4 tablespoonfuls of caster sugar. Add vanilla to taste, and continue to beat until smooth and creamy. Butter a mould (a small cake tin will do) and line it with greaseproof paper. Press the mixture well in. Put in the fridge to set. Turn out on to a dish and serve with whipped cream.

SWEETS WITH WHOLE EGGS

PROFITEROLLES AU CHOCOLAT

This is much less complicated than it sounds, but it does take quite a time to prepare. The profiterolles can be made the day before, and the filling added an hour or so before serving.

Start by making some pâte à choux (for 4 people halve the quantities given on page 114), and put heaped teaspoonfuls on to a greased baking sheet—not too close together, as they swell in cooking. Brush with beaten egg and bake in a hot oven (Reg. 6) for 20–30 minutes. Take out and cool on a wire tray, then make an incision in each profiterolle and fill with a crème pâtissière (see the recipe on page 125). Arrange in a pile on a dish, and when ready to serve pour over a hot chocolate sauce.

For the sauce, put into a saucepan three-quarters of a

tumbler of water and ¼ lb. tablet of unsweetened chocolate. When melted, add 3 dessertspoonfuls of caster sugar and stir until smooth. Dissolve a tablespoonful of cornflour in half a glass of water and add little by little to the chocolate mixture. You may not need to add all. The sauce should be thick, but not unmanageably 'gooey'. Bring to the boil, simmer for a minute or two, pour over the profiterolles and serve at once.

NÈGRE EN CHEMISE

Although I did not intend to include any classic recipes in this book, I feel that I cannot omit this most famous of sweets, as it is easy to prepare and looks festive and attractive at the end of a meal.

Melt 6 oz. unsweetened chocolate in a tablespoonful of strong coffee and beat into it the same quantity of butter. When smooth add, away from the fire, the yolks of 3 eggs and make sure they are properly amalgamated. Whip the whites stiffly and fold gently into the mixture. Pour into an oiled mould and leave in the fridge until the next day. Unmould before serving and cover with whipped cream.

MOUSSE AU CHOCOLAT

The omission of the butter in this recipe makes it lighter than the previous one. It is a delicious, easy and quick sweet to make when eggs are cheap and gives a very professional round-off to a dinner party.

Allow 1 oz. unsweetened chocolate and 1 egg per person (with perhaps an additional couple for second helpings). Melt the chocolate slowly in a saucepan, with a little coffee. For 6 eggs and 6 oz. chocolate, 2 tablespoonfuls of coffee should be about right. Separate the yolks and the whites. Beat up the yolks and add to the melted chocolate, together with 2 tablespoonfuls of sugar and a teaspoonful of vanilla essence. Then add the whites whipped very stiffly, and fold the mixture gently over and over till perfectly amalgamated. Put into a glass dish, decorate the top with chopped nuts and leave in the fridge to set. It should be eaten very cold.

COLD ORANGE SOUFFLÉ

Beat together 4 tablespoonfuls of sugar and the yolks of 4 eggs in the top of a double saucepan. When light and frothy, add 2 teacupfuls of milk and cook over gently boiling water till the custard thickens. Melt a tablespoonful of powdered gelatine in a little water and add to the cooled custard with 2 teacupfuls of orange juice and a tablespoonful of grated orange peel. Beat the whites of the eggs stiffly and fold gently into the mixture. Pour into a glass dish and leave to set in the fridge. Just before serving, sprinkle the top with sparsely-grated chocolate.

COLD NUT SOUFFLÉ

Beat the yolks of 2 eggs with 3 tablespoonfuls of sugar. Pour on $\frac{1}{4}$ pint of milk and bring to the boil. Dissolve a level tablespoonful of powdered gelatine in water and stir into the custard. Whisk the egg whites to stiff peaks and fold carefully in, then 3 tablespoonfuls of cream and lastly 4 tablespoonfuls of ground skinned walnuts. (Shell the walnuts and dip them into boiling water, when the skins will come off quite easily. Grind them in the cheese grater.)

This is a most unusual-tasting sweet. When walnuts are not in season, you can use hazel nuts—but not almonds, which are too oily and too strongly flavoured.

GÂTEAU DE FROMAGE BLANC

Put the yolks of 2 eggs into the top of a double boiler. Add 2 tablespoonfuls of caster sugar, 2 level tablespoonfuls of powdered gelatine, ½ pint of orange juice, and a pinch of salt, and simmer till the gelatine is dissolved. In the meantime sieve ½ lb. cottage cheese. Stir the mixture in the saucepan and as it begins to thicken remove from the heat and add the sieved cheese, a tablespoonful of grated orange rind and ½ pint of stiffly-whipped cream. Whisk the egg whites into peaks, then add 2 tablespoonfuls of sugar. Whisk again till stiff, then fold into the cheese mixture. Pour into a tin rinsed with cold water, and chill in the fridge. To serve, turn out on to a flat dish and decorate with grated biscuit crumbs (digestive biscuits are excellent), or if you prefer, use grated chocolate.

LEMON FLUFF

As children, this used to be almost our favourite sweet, and it was invariably served on our birthdays.

Put half a breakfast cup of caster sugar, 1 breakfast cup of water and the juice of 2 lemons into a saucepan and bring to the boil. Mix 3 dessertspoonfuls of cornflour with a little water and add to the liquid in the saucepan. Boil gently, stirring continuously for 2 minutes. Remove from the heat. Whip the whites of 2 eggs to a stiff froth, fold them into the mixture, then pour it into a wetted mould and chill. To serve, unmould and pour over it a crème anglaise made from the 2 egg yolks, a heaped tablespoonful of caster sugar and a ½ pint of milk (for the method see the recipe on page 125).

OEUFS À LA NEIGE

Beat the whites of 3 eggs very stiffly and mix with 3 tablespoonfuls of caster sugar. Boil some water in a fairly deep saucepan, then turn down the heat and drop in the egg whites by tablespoonfuls. Don't let the water boil again. When one side is cooked, turn over with a perforated slice. The cooking should take about 3 minutes. Drain on to a clean cloth, and leave to cool. Serve floating on a vanilla-flavoured crème anglaise, made with the yolks of the eggs, 3 tablespoonfuls of caster sugar and ½ pint of milk (see page 125). You can decorate each 'half egg' with a spoonful of strawberry or raspberry jam.

CRÈMES FRITES

Although these creams have to be cooked at the last moment, this only takes 5 minutes and the mixture can be prepared in advance. What little delay there may be is well worth the waiting.

Beat together in a saucepan 2 whole eggs, 3 tablespoonfuls of sugar and a teaspoonful of vanilla essence. When well mixed and frothy, add a heaped teaspoonful of flour and a heaped tablespoonful of ground rice. Now pour in a pint of boiling milk. Stir continually till the mixture has well thickened. Pour it into a buttered dish and spread it, with a palette knife, about an inch thick. Let it get quite cold, then cut it into rounds of about 1½ inches in diameter. Roll these in flour, dip in beaten egg, and afterwards roll in breadcrumbs, and fry in very hot oil till crisp.

PAIN PERDU

This is a most excellent way of using up stale bread.

For 4 people stir 5 tablespoonfuls of caster sugar into a pint of milk, then beat up 2 eggs and add the sweetened milk to them. Dip the pieces of bread in the milk and egg—but don't saturate them or they will disintegrate when you take them out. They should be just coated. Fry in very hot oil, when they should puff up. Drain on soft paper and serve with a syrup made from a wineglass of white wine and a spoonful of sugar, and flavoured with grated lemon peel and a pinch of ground cinnamon.

POTATO PUDDING

The following two recipes came out of a ladies' magazine of the late nineteenth century, and they are so typical of English cooking at its best that I thought they should be included in this entente cordiale of recipes.

'Boil 1 lb. potatoes till soft, drain well and rub them through a sieve. While still hot beat in ¼ lb. butter. Beat up the yolks of 4 whole eggs and the whites of two. Add ¼ lb. of white sugar, ¼ pint of white wine, and stir them well together. Grate in half a nutmeg and stir in ¼ pint thick cream. Pour the mixture into a pie dish and bake till golden brown.'

I find that half a nutmeg is too much, and I advise you to taste your mixture when you have incorporated half that amount. I allow the pudding to bake for half an hour (Reg. 6). Have a look, and if it is not golden and crisp leave it in for another 10 minutes.

WALMER PUDDING

This is quite a good, and not at all stodgy, hot sweet, which can be left to cook while you are having your main course. It makes a good finish to a cold supper.

Melt 2 oz. butter in a saucepan, and when beginning to bubble add 2½ tablespoonfuls of flour. Stir continuously, adding sufficient milk to make the mixture the consistency of thick cream. Remove from the heat and cool for a few minutes, then beat in a tablespoonful of caster sugar, a tea-spoonful of vanilla essence and the yolks of 2 eggs. Whip the whites very stiff (they should stand in little peaks) and fold into the mixture in the saucepan. Do not beat any more. Spread a layer of strawberry or apricot jam at the bottom of a pie dish. Pour the pudding mixture on to it and bake in a hot oven (Reg. 6) for 15–20 minutes. The pudding should be well risen and golden when done.

SWEETS WITH EGG YOLKS

CRÈME ANGLAISE

Neither this nor the following recipe can, I suppose, be really called a sweet, as they are usually served as an accompaniment to something else. But they make a light finish to a menu in which the main course has been substantial, and look attractive if served in individual glasses.

For crème anglaise, beat the yolks of 4 eggs with 2 tablespoonfuls of caster sugar till light and frothy. They should be almost white. Pour in a pint of milk. Turn into the top of your double boiler and cook gently until the cream has thickened. Stir frequently. Chill and strain before serving the cream which can be flavoured with vanilla, orange, lemon or coffee.

These quantities make quite a large amount.

CRÈME PÂTISSIÈRE

Beat, in a saucepan, the yolks of 3 eggs with 4 tablespoonfuls of caster sugar till white and frothy, add 2 tablespoonfuls of flour and, when well mixed, ¾ pint of boiling milk. Bring to the boil, stirring all the time, and allow to thicken. Chill before serving.

CAFÉ PARFAIT

In the top half of a double saucepan boil a teacupful of strong coffee with ¾ cupful of caster sugar till syrupy (about 5 minutes). Remove from the heat. Beat the yolks of 4 eggs and add to the coffee syrup. Cook over gently boiling water, stirring constantly, until the mixture coats the back of the spoon. Remove from the heat, cool, and add a pinch of salt and 1½ teaspoonfuls of vanilla essence. Whip ½ pint of cream till stiff and fold into the cooled syrup. Leave in the fridge at least an hour, before serving in individual dishes.

PETITS POTS DE CRÈME À LA VANILLE

Bring a pint of milk to the boil with 3 tablespoonfuls of caster sugar. Stir the sugar well in, remove from the heat and allow to get cold. Add 1 teaspoonful of vanilla essence. Beat the yolks of 4 eggs and incorporate with the milk. Strain into little fireproof pots, put them in a baking tin with water in it and cook in the oven (Reg. 5) for 30–45 minutes. Neither the water nor the custard must boil.

GÂTEAU VIENNOIS

This sweet requires no cooking, but it is best to make it the day before you want to eat it.

Cream together 4 oz. butter and 2 tablespoonfuls of caster sugar. Add the yolks of 4 eggs, a tablespoonful of strong coffee, 4 oz. unsweetened chocolate, grated, and 10 tablespoonfuls of stale breadcrumbs. (This is a good way to use up a stale loaf.) Mix well together and put into a small cake tin or soufflé dish, pressing the mixture well down. Leave to set in the fridge. To serve, turn out and cover the top with whipped cream.

SWEETS WITH EGG WHITES

VISITANDINES

If you have made a mayonnaise, here is a good way to use up your egg whites.

Mix in a basin 4 tablespoonfuls of sieved flour, 8 tablespoonfuls of caster sugar, 3 tablespoonfuls of ground almonds and the grated peel of a lemon. Beat the whites of 5 eggs very stiffly and fold into the mixture. Melt ¼ lb. butter, but do not let it boil. Pour it on to your egg and flour mixture, stirring till it is well amalgamated. Butter little moulds, and spoon the mixture in. Do not fill more than two-thirds high, as it will rise in the cooking. Bake in a moderate oven (Reg. 4) for half an hour. Leave for a moment or two before turning out. Serve with a jam sauce or a crème anglaise (see page 125).

FINANCIERS

Beat 3½ oz. butter to a cream. Beat the whites of 4 eggs with 5 tablespoonfuls of caster sugar for at least 20 minutes. Add 3 heaped tablespoonfuls of flour and the creamed butter. Stir gently, folding the whites carefully into the flour and butter. Butter some small fireproof pots. Half fill with the mixture and bake for 20 minutes in a moderate oven (Reg. 5). Turn out on to the centre of a dish and decorate with quarters of crystallized oranges or lemons.

Sweets

MOUSSE AU CHOCOLAT

Whisk the whites of 6 eggs till stiff and peaky. Melt 6 oz. unsweetened chocolate in 2 tablespoonfuls of orange juice. Add sugar to taste. You should now have a thick sauce. Fold in the whites, turning over and over till perfectly mixed, spoon into a glass dish and chill. You will find the slight orange flavour a change from vanilla or coffee.

FLAMÉRI DE SEMOULE

Cook 4 tablespoonfuls of semolina in a pint of milk. When well thickened, stir in 3 tablespoonfuls of caster sugar and a dessertspoonful of powdered gelatine dissolved in a little water. Bring to the boil again and fold in the whites of 3 eggs, beaten stiffly. Rinse out a mould in cold water and fill with the mixture. Chill in the fridge. When you want to eat it, turn out on to a shallow dish, decorate with glacé fruits and pour round some redcurrant jelly diluted in a little water or liqueur, such as kirsch. A most appetizing and very inexpensive sweet.

MOUSSE AUX FRAISES

This is a strawberry mousse with a difference and a perfect sweet to make when strawberries are cheap and getting towards the end of their season.

Put a pound of strawberries through a sieve, and mix them with 2 tablespoonfuls of sugar and ½ pint of stiffly-whipped cream. (In the summer cream, too, is cheaper.) Put this mixture into a glass dish, or individual glasses. Now beat the whites of 4 eggs till stiff and peaky. Add a tablespoonful of sieved icing sugar and 2 tablespoonfuls of grated chocolate. Top the strawberry mixture with the chocolate and egg foam, and decorate with fresh strawberries.

Ideas for Apéritif Parties

Potato sticks • Cheese sablés • Danish dip • Choux surprises • Sweet and sour sticks • Gnocchis au fromage • Pruneaux farcis • Potato balls • Dolmades • Humous bi Tahina • Canapés de pain d'épice • Bowle • Rum punch • Mint julep • Mexican drink

Ideas for Apéritif Parties

All the following recipes can be prepared in advance and finished on the day. I know there are countless mouth-watering cocktail specialities on sale at most of the big stores, but really nothing replaces freshly-made, home-produced savouries.

POTATO STICKS

Boil a pound of potatoes and sieve them. While still hot, put 6 tablespoonfuls of the purée into a warmed bowl and beat in 6 oz. butter. Now work in 6 tablespoonfuls of flour, with plenty of salt and pepper. It will probably be rather sticky, so wrap in foil and allow to rest in the fridge. When you are ready to cook the sticks, roll out the paste to $\frac{1}{4}$ in. thickness, brush over with beaten egg and dust with caraway seeds. Cut into little sticks and bake in a moderate oven until brown and crisp.

CHEESE SABLÉS

Cream 4 oz. butter in a bowl, with a wooden spoon, then work in 4 tablespoonfuls of grated cheese and 8 tablespoon-fuls of flour. Roll into a ball, wrap in foil and put in the fridge until wanted. To cook, roll out thinly on a floured board and cut either into little rounds or into sticks. Arrange in a baking tray and cook in the oven (Reg. 6) for 5–7 minutes. They should be just coloured. Remove on to a wire tray and cool before putting them away. They will keep indefinitely in a tin.

DANISH DIP

Buy a jar of red caviare (about 4s. 6d.) and beat it into $\frac{1}{4}$ lb. cream cheese. Add lemon juice and pepper but no salt, as the caviare is very salty. Serve with plenty of fingers of toast or little rectangular biscuits.

CHOUX SURPRISES

Remove the rind from 6 rashers of bacon and cut each rasher into three. Beat 6 oz. cottage or cream cheese with 2 tablespoonfuls of chopped walnuts. Season with freshly-ground black pepper. Put a spoonful of the filling on each piece of bacon and roll up. Make some choux paste (see page 114), and put teaspoonfuls on a baking sheet (following the instructions for profiterolles on page 119). When the buns are cooled, fill them with the little bacon rolls and put back in the oven (Reg. 5) for 10 minutes. Can be served cold, but better hot.

SWEET AND SOUR STICKS

For summer parties, you will have enormous success if you serve a pile of cocktail sticks each speared with a cube of pineapple between one of cheddar cheese and one of cucumber.

GNOCCHIS AU FROMAGE

Although these sound rather messy, they can be eaten in your fingers; but spear them on cocktail sticks if you prefer.

Make a pâte à choux (see page 114). Let it cool and then roll it into a long narrow sausage on a floured board. Cut it into pieces about half an inch thick. Have some salted water on the boil. Put a small handful of the gnocchis into the water and allow to simmer for 10 minutes. Take out and drain. When all the gnocchis are cooked, arrange them on a fireproof dish and sprinkle with ¼ lb. of grated cheese (Gruyère for preference), and salt and pepper, then sprinkle with 2 oz. melted butter. Put into a very hot oven (Reg. 9) for 10 minutes. Keep hot until required.

PRUNEAUX FARCIS

Soak some prunes in half red wine and half water for an hour or so. Cook them gently, without sugar, till soft. Take them out and drain well. Remove the stones and stuff the prunes with cream cheese and chopped olives. Roll little rashers of streaky bacon round the stuffed prunes and grill on both sides till crisp. Serve on cocktail sticks.

POTATO BALLS

Peel 1 lb. potatoes and boil in salted water, drain and pass through a sieve. While still warm, add an ounce of butter with pepper and a grating of nutmeg. Form little balls with your floured hands and dip them in an egg white beaten to a froth with a dessertspoonful of oil. Then roll them in crisp breadcrumbs and fry in very hot oil. Drain on soft paper and keep warm until wanted.

DOLMADES

These are the famous Greek stuffed vine leaves which, with slight variations, are served in all Eastern Mediterranean countries as an hors-d'oeuvre. One of the principal herbs used in the North of Africa and the Near East is mint—in fact one of its main uses is as an infusion, and it is a most refreshing one. The following recipe, to have the authentic flavour, should contain a little chopped mint.

Buy ½ lb. vine leaves, either loose or in a tin. In either case, drain them and spread them out on a table. Chop a small onion and fry it in oil. Mix it, with the oil, into a breakfast cupful of cooked rice and stir in a little grated nutmeg, a pinch of cinnamon and a little chopped mint (dried, if you cannot get fresh). Put on each leaf a spoonful of the spiced rice, using a coffee spoon for the small leaves, a teaspoon for the larger ones, and fold the leaves into little parcels with the ends tucked in. Arrange them carefully in layers in a shallow fireproof dish, squeeze lemon juice over them and add a tablespoonful of tomato purée dissolved in stock or water (enough to come to the top of the bottom layer). Cover, and cook very gently for half an hour. Serve very cold, piled in a glass dish.

HUMOUS BI TAHINA

This is also served as an hors-d'oeuvre, in North Africa, and is usually eaten with hot flat bread. It makes an excellent dip for a buffet party.

Soak ½ lb. chick peas overnight, and then simmer for several hours. They must be soft enough to put through the food mill. When this has been done, stir the juice of half a lemon, a teacupful of oil (olive oil if you have it), salt and pepper, a teacupful of Tahina (which is a paste made from sesame seeds, and which you can buy in the sort of Oriental stores which stock spices for curries), a handful of chopped mint, and a pounded clove of garlic (optional). Add water to thin out the mixture. It should be like a creamy purée. Serve in a shallow glass dish, with slices of crusty French bread.

CANAPÉS DE PAIN D'ÉPICE

Although pain d'épice isn't strictly speaking a thing to be served as an appetizer, it can, however, with the addition of a cream cheese and olive spread, make a delicious canapé which goes very well with sherry and punch.

For the pain d'épice (the traditional spiced bread eaten all over France), sieve into a basin 12 tablespoonfuls of flour, 2 tablespoonfuls of brown sugar, 1 teaspoonful of powdered cinnamon, 1 teaspoonful of powdered ginger, 1 teaspoonful of bicarbonate of soda, and a pinch of salt. Rub in 4 oz. butter until quite free from lumps. Shred into the mixture the rind of an orange. Now pour in 2 tablespoonfuls of golden syrup and 2 tablespoonfuls of honey (previously warmed) and the strained juice of the orange. Add warm water until the mixture becomes of a consistency that will just drop from the spoon. Beat well for a few minutes, then pour into a well greased sandwich or flat cake tin. Bake in a slow oven (Reg. 3) for 45 minutes, when it should be well risen and firm to the touch. Turn out on a sieve and leave till cool. It should keep well if stored in a tin. To serve with apéritifs, cut into small squares and spread thickly with cream cheese into which you have mixed chopped stuffed olives and a little chopped gherkin.

I want to end this chapter with a few inexpensive drinks.

BOWLE

In the summer, serve a Bowle, which you can make several

hours before you need it and which is deliciously cool and refreshing.

Soak some peaches (fresh if possible, but tinned ones will do quite well) in brandy. To a third of a bottle of brandy you will need 4 bottles of white wine. You can buy a cheap one, but don't get it too dry. Leave on ice until required, and then pour in a bottle of champagne or sparkling muscatel. Serve very cold.

RUM PUNCH

Here is a winter drink, which you can dilute with more water if it seems too strong.

For 2 quarts of punch you will need half a bottle of brandy, half a bottle of rum, 3 pints of water, a large lemon, 3 oz. loaf sugar, and a pinch of ground cinnamon, a grating of nutmeg and a clove. Remove the zest of the lemon by rubbing it with some of the sugar. Put all the sugar and the brandy, rum and spices into a saucepan with the water. Heat so that the sugar is melted and well mixed. Keep warm until required. To serve, strain the juice of the lemon into a big bowl, pour the hot liquid over and serve with a ladle. It must not boil.

MINT JULEP

This is a famous American drink which used to be much served in the hot southern States. It is delicious for a summer party.

Boil a bunch of mint with sugar and water until the flavour is extracted. When cool, strain into a jug, add ice, and for each pint of extract add ⅓ pint of brandy. Stir up well. To serve, pour into iced tumblers, in which are 2 or 3 sprigs of mint moistened and dipped in caster sugar, and dash a few drops of rum on the top. To be made at the last moment.

MEXICAN DRINK

And for those of you who do not like any alcoholic drink, here is a piquant and refreshing thirst-quencher.

Strain equal quantities of orange and pineapple juice and add the juice of a lemon to each pint of liquid, then add grated orange peel and crushed mint leaves. Stand overnight in a cool place. When ready to serve, put some ice cubes at the bottom of a jug, pour in the juice, add caster sugar and a dash of cinnamon to taste, and top with a sprig of mint.

Sauces

Béchamel • Sauce Mornay • Sauce Poulette • Sauce Espagnole • Tomato sauce • Sauce Béarnaise • Sauce Hollandaise • Sauce Vinaigrette • Sauce à l'orange • Cranberry sauce • Mayonnaise • Sauce Tartare • Sauce Rémoulade • Aïoli • Sauce chasseur • Marinade • Court bouillon

Sauces

❖❖❖

Do not think that it will be a waste of time to read this chapter. Sauces are not the complicated preparations that so many people seem to think, and once you understand the principles of thickening the different categories, you will find that every sauce is a variant of one or other of them.

By far the greatest number of hot sauces are those thickened with a roux—that is, with a basis of flour cooked in fat—and thinned to the correct consistency by the addition of liquid.

Roux are either white, blond (in which the flour and fat are cooked until golden), or brown (in which you continue the cooking until the paste has darkened and has acquired a slightly nutty flavour). To make a roux, melt the fat in the saucepan and stir in the flour till the mixture is smooth and bubbling. At this moment you start adding your liquid, still stirring, until it is of the correct creamy texture. For a brown roux you must not start adding your liquid until the flour and fat have reached the right colour.

The next category is liquids thickened with either starch, egg, butter or cream. Starch (i.e. flour, cornflour, ground rice or breadcrumbs) gives only body to a liquid without adding anything to the flavour.

Egg yolk added to a liquid and slowly heated will thicken and give an unctuous but light quality to your sauce.

Butter or cream added to a liquid form an emulsion and give consistency and savour to a sauce. The fat must be well

141

beaten into the hot liquid, but never boiled or it will separate. The sauce should be served immediately.

The last category of sauces are those called emulsified sauces, the most classic example of which is, of course, mayonnaise. This category includes Béarnaise and Hollandaise sauces, and, though the most tricky to make, once you have the knack you should find no difficulty in achieving success every time.

BÉCHAMEL

This is the sauce which forms the basis of all sauces in which fat, flour and liquid are the principal ingredients.

Melt 1 oz. butter in a saucepan, and when foaming, stir in a heaped tablespoonful of flour. When thoroughly amalgamated add, away from the fire, $\frac{1}{2}$ to $\frac{1}{3}$ pint of liquid—milk or stock. Season with salt and pepper and put back on the fire, stirring until it thickens. It should look creamy. Cook for a further 10 minutes.

SAUCE MORNAY

Make a Béchamel with a white roux and flavour with cheese and a scrape of grated nutmeg.

SAUCE POULETTE

An excellent sauce to serve with fish.

Make a Béchamel, using the stock from a court bouillon (see page 148) with the addition of the juice of a lemon and, if you like, a wineglassful of white wine. It should be thin and creamy.

SAUCE ESPAGNOLE

This, with slight variations, will enrich any game or red meat dish.

Make a brown roux over a slow fire—this is important as otherwise you will get a burnt taste. Moisten with meat stock (use a bouillon cube if you have no home-made stock). While this is simmering, fry in another saucepan a small onion, a small diced carrot, and 2 or 3 tomatoes. Add a small glass of sherry or white wine, salt and pepper and a bouquet of herbs. When the vegetables have taken colour and are soft, put through the food mill into the sauce and continue cooking for a further 20–30 minutes. Strain before serving.

TOMATO SAUCE

Cut up a pound of ripe tomatoes and put them in a pan with a chopped clove of garlic, salt, pepper, a teaspoonful of sugar and a pinch of dried basil. Cook very slowly with the lid on the pan (about 20 minutes) and when soft and pulpy, put through a sieve.

SAUCE BÉARNAISE

If you can make a custard in a double saucepan, there is absolutely no reason why you should quail at the thought of Sauce Béarnaise, usually considered the acmé of cordon bleu cooking. Remember only that the water in the bottom of the saucepan must never boil, and that you must stir the sauce continually.

Into the top half of the saucepan put 2 chopped shallots (or a small onion), a branch of tarragon (or $\frac{1}{2}$ teaspoonful of dried leaves if you have no fresh), a sprig of parsley, a little ground pepper and half a tumbler of vinegar. Boil this fiercely until it is reduced by two-thirds. Strain into a basin (reserve the liquid), and add a teaspoonful of cold water. Put into the top half of your saucepan the yolks of 4 eggs well beaten. Now add the vinegar liquid and a nut of butter. Replace the saucepan on to the lower half and start cooking very gently over hot water. As the mixture starts to thicken, add little bits of butter until you have incorporated 4 oz., by which time the sauce should be done. Once cooked, don't put it back on the fire. Leave it over the hot water and serve tepid.

SAUCE HOLLANDAISE

This is the same idea as in the previous recipe. Mix a tablespoonful of vinegar and 2 tablespoonfuls of water, with a pinch of pepper and salt, and reduce by two-thirds. Cook for a minute and then add gradually over hot water the yolks of 4 eggs and stir until thickened. Remove from the heat and, keeping the saucepan over the hot water, add 6 oz. butter in small pieces. Stir in a little lemon juice and another spoonful of cold water.

SAUCE VINAIGRETTE

(See also page 19.)

The classic oil and vinegar dressing used for salads can be dressed up with herbs, parsley, and a teaspoonful of finely-chopped onion or shallot, to be served with certain kinds of brawn and cold meats.

SAUCE À L'ORANGE

Try this very piquant sauce with hot ham, roast pork or roast duck. It is also very good with cold meat.

You need 2 teaspoonfuls of horseradish sauce, the juice of 2 oranges and the grated rind of 1 orange, a teaspoonful of caster sugar, a pinch of salt and 2 tablespoonfuls of redcurrant jelly. Mix all together in a saucepan and warm slightly in order to amalgamate the jelly with the other ingredients. Chill before serving.

CRANBERRY SAUCE

Put 1 lb. cranberries in a saucepan with a teacupful of cold water. Bring to the boil and stew until reduced to pulp, bruising them well with a fork or the back of a wooden spoon. Beat in 4 tablespoonfuls of sugar and chill before serving.

MAYONNAISE

Nothing tastes quite like a freshly-made mayonnaise. It is supposed to be difficult to make, which is why so many amateur cooks avoid it. But if you are prepared to spend ten minutes or a quarter of an hour on it, and take the following precautions, you should be sure of success every time.

The element which causes the sauce to bind is the salt, so don't be afraid to use what may seem a large quantity for the amount of sauce you are going to make.

I have found that, in spite of all that has been written about never using eggs which have just come out of the fridge, the temperature of the eggs is immaterial, but on the other hand it is important to use oil at room temperature.

The secret of a successful mayonnaise is to beat the yolks well with the salt, so that they have already begun to thicken before you start adding the oil—drop by drop at first, till the sauce has taken on its well-known shiny consistency, and then by teaspoonfuls. But be sure one lot of oil is thoroughly incorporated before adding the next. When the sauce is really thick and stiff, add a very little vinegar to thin it down, and when finished pour in a spoonful of boiling water. This cooks the egg and prevents the sauce acquiring a skin if it is not to be used at once. If, in spite of all your precautions, your sauce turns, don't throw it away. Put a spoonful of boiling water into a clean basin, and beat into it, drop by drop, the curdled mixture. Continue to beat until the sauce is completely amalgamated again, then proceed as before.

Now for the method. For 4 people break the yolks of 2 eggs into a basin with ½ teaspoonful of salt and ½ coffee-spoonful of pepper. Stir briskly until the mixture starts to thicken. I always use a wooden spoon, but many people find they get better results with an egg whisk, or even a fork. Then add, as described in the previous paragraph, the oil and vinegar—about ½ pint of oil to a teaspoonful of vinegar.

SAUCE TARTARE

This is a stiff mayonnaise to which you add chopped capers, parsley, chives, tarragon and a little gherkin.

SAUCE RÉMOULADE

Pound the yolk of a hard-boiled egg with a little mustard, mix with the yolk of a raw egg and continue as for a mayonnaise, adding salt and oil. When made, stir in chopped parsley, chives and capers.

AÏOLI

Aïoli is another variation of mayonnaise, eaten in the Provence district. Its principal characteristic is the addition of garlic. Crush 2 cloves of garlic, and on to them break 2 egg yolks. Add salt and pepper and a slice of bread soaked in milk and squeezed dry. Mix well together then add ½ pint of oil, a few drops at a time. Thin out with lemon juice.

SAUCE CHASSEUR

A very good sharp sauce to serve with any sauté of meat. Make a marinade with a glass of white wine, a tablespoon of oil and the juice of a lemon. Chop into it 2 shallots, season with pepper, parsley and thyme. Leave for an hour, then reduce by fast boiling to two-thirds of its original volume. Make a brown roux with 2 oz. butter, and a good tablespoonful of flour, moistening it with the marinade and if possible the juice from a roast. Simmer for 30 minutes and add before serving 2 tablespoonfuls of redcurrant jelly.

The last two recipes are not, strictly speaking, sauces; but as they frequently form the basis of sauces I thought it better to include them in this chapter.

MARINADE

To marinate fish or meat is to soak it in a mixture of wine, oil, and herbs so that it becomes impregnated. The toughest piece of stewing meat will become tender after being left for an hour or two in a marinade before cooking. I give here a basic recipe with red wine, but there are infinite variations. This is a fairly representative version. The amount of marinade you make depends, of course, on the amount of meat or fish you are going to soak in it.

To a pint of red wine add a teaspoonful of vinegar. Add 2 carrots, cut into large pieces, and 2 onions, sliced, with peppercorns, a clove or two, a clove of garlic, a branch of thyme, a bay leaf and some parsley stalks. Turn the meat over from time to time, so that every part of it becomes impregnated. When ready to cook, strain the marinade and throw away the vegetables and herbs which will have become tasteless and mushy. Lay fresh vegetables in your casserole, put in the meat, and pour the marinade over. This is the principle for making slow beef stews.

COURT BOUILLON

This is a fish stock and forms the basis of many fish dishes.

To a pint of water add half a bottle of dry white wine, 2 carrots chopped roughly, 2 onions sliced, and a bouquet of parsley, thyme and bay leaf, with salt, peppercorns and a few cloves. Cover and simmer for half an hour, then strain and put aside till required. It will keep at least 24 hours in the fridge.

A Guide for Comparative Weights and Liquid Measures

	Level teaspoon	Level tablespoon
Flour	$\frac{1}{4}$ oz.	$\frac{1}{3}$ oz.
Caster sugar	$\frac{1}{4}$ oz.	$\frac{1}{2}$ oz.
Rice		$\frac{3}{4}$ oz.
Grated cheese		$\frac{1}{3}$ oz.

	Heaped teaspoon	Heaped tablespoon
Flour	$\frac{1}{3}$ oz.	1 oz.
Caster sugar	$\frac{1}{3}$ oz.	1 oz.
Rice		$1\frac{1}{2}$ oz.
Grated cheese		1 oz.

1 tumbler	$\frac{1}{2}$ pint
6 tablespoonfuls water	2 fluid oz. ($\frac{1}{2}$ gill)
1 teacup	$\frac{1}{4}$ pint (5 oz.)

Comparative Oven Temperatures

GAS	ELECTRICITY
$\frac{1}{4}$	240
$\frac{1}{2}$	260
1	290
2	300
3	330
4	350
5	380
6	400
7	420
8	430
9	450
10	470
	500

Index

Index

Index